"In a world of blustering, rumpus, platform-infatuated pastors and writers, it is both joy and balm to encounter a pastor who knows the way of beauty (both with sentences and with people). These pages do what good writers and good pastors are supposed to do: open the world's doors wide, beckon us out, and help us revel in all the wonder and holiness. We need more of these kinds of words in the world."

—WINN COLLIER
Director, Eugene Peterson Center for Christian Imagination

"Good reading ennobles us, gives us the imaginative resources to scale what Rilke called 'the mountains of the heart.' Doug Basler knows this. Knows that curious, attentive, deep reading has the power to put us in conversation with our own lives in ways that might bring about what the New Testament calls metanoia—a changing of the mind that changes everything. *All Swirling and Weaving* is a valuable witness and apprenticeship to this critical skill. Highly recommended."

—ANDREW ARNDT
Lead Pastor, New Life East

"As Flannery O'Connor might have said, a good pastor is hard to find. But we've found a fine one in Douglas Basler, both in his service and in his writing. As you taste his reflections on the novels that undergird his ministry, you will not just want to read these works of fiction yourself; you will also want to emulate Doug Basler's care for the ragged souls that are all around us—and within."

—PAUL J. WILLIS
Author of *To Build a Trail*

"The first time I heard Doug read an excerpt of an essay that would appear in this book was at a reading one night near Lake Michigan. The tone of the room changed after Doug started to read, because he has a clear, understated, and profound way of merging ideas and context. Suddenly, we were all paying attention. Like that first reading, I loved this writing. *All Swirling All Weaving* gives readers permission to slow down, be present, and take notice. In a frenetic and divided culture, this book is a gulp of fresh water. This collection meets readers where we are in a voice that is personal, pastoral, and profoundly human."

—SARA BILLUPS
Author of *Nervous Systems*

All Swirling and Weaving

All Swirling and Weaving

Reflections on Reading Fiction and Growing in Faith

DOUGLAS BASLER

Foreword by Marilyn McEntyre

WIPF & STOCK · Eugene, Oregon

ALL SWIRLING AND WEAVING
Reflections on Reading Fiction and Growing in Faith

Copyright © 2025 Douglas Basler. All rights reserved. Except for brief quotations in critical publications or reviews, no part of this book may be reproduced in any manner without prior written permission from the publisher. Write: Permissions, Wipf and Stock Publishers, 199 W. 8th Ave., Suite 3, Eugene, OR 97401.

Wipf & Stock
An Imprint of Wipf and Stock Publishers
199 W. 8th Ave., Suite 3
Eugene, OR 97401

www.wipfandstock.com

PAPERBACK ISBN: 979-8-3852-5382-1
HARDCOVER ISBN: 979-8-3852-5383-8
EBOOK ISBN: 979-8-3852-5384-5

VERSION NUMBER 092925

Unless otherwise indicated, Scripture quotations are from The Holy Bible, New International Version®, NIV®. Copyright © 2011 by Biblica, Inc. Used with permission of Zondervan. All rights reserved worldwide. www.zondervan.com.

Scripture quotations marked (NRSV) are from the New Revised Standard Version Updated Edition. Copyright © 2021 National Council of Churches of Christ in the United States of America. Used by permission. All rights reserved worldwide.

Scripture quotations marked (KJV) are from the Authorized (King James) Version. Rights in the Authorized Version in the United Kingdom are vested in the Crown. Reproduced by permission of the Crown's patentee, Cambridge University Press.

Scripture quotations marked (ESV) are from The ESV® Bible (The Holy Bible, English Standard Version®), © 2001 by Crossway, a publishing ministry of Good News Publishers. Used by permission. All rights reserved.

An abridged version of the chapter "All Swirling and Braiding and Weaving and Spinning" was first published online in *Ekstasis* as "The Poetry of a Pastor," December 14, 2023. It is reprinted here with permission.

An abridged version of the chapter "Ruin Was Part of the Draw" was first published in *The Presbyterian Outlook* as "Closing a Church Faithfully," Vol. 205, No. 7, July/August 2023. It is reprinted here with permission.

Excerpts of the chapter "Drawn from a Different Well" were first published in *The Presbyterian Outlook* as "Taking a Stand on Unity," Vol. 206, No. 2, February 2024. These excerpts are reprinted here with permission.

To the Useless Pastors

"…our mouths were filled with laughter"
—Psalm 126:2

And to the congregations of Mt. Republic Chapel of Peace
and First Presbyterian Church of Aberdeen

"I thank my God every time I remember you"
—Philippians 1:3

Contents

Foreword | ix

Acknowledgments | xi

Introduction | xiii

On Reading and Pastoring: Claire Keegan's *Small Things like These* | 1

All Swirling and Braiding and Weaving and Spinning:
   Brian Doyle's *Mink River* | 9

Ruin Was Part of the Draw: Leif Enger's *Virgil Wander* | 18

A Hundred Books Could Not Capture a Single Village:
   Niall Williams's *This Is Happiness* | 28

The Membership: Wendell Berry's *Nathan Coulter* | 36

Drawn from a Different Well:
   James McBride's *The Heaven and Earth Grocery Store* | 44

Onesies and Twosies: Barbara Kingsolver's *The Bean Trees* | 53

One Foot in Front of the Other: Alice McDermott's *The Ninth Hour* | 63

Circles and Circles of Sorrow: Toni Morrison's *Sula* | 74

They Did Indeed Move in a Mysterious Way:
   David James Duncan's *The Brothers K* | 85

The World Was All Before Them, Such as It Was:
   Marilynne Robinson's *Jack* | 95

Playful Excess: Andrew Peterson's *The Wingfeather Saga* | 106

Bibliography | 119

Foreword

It takes a lively imagination to suggest that stories are "part of the air we breathe—the atmosphere we create among us." That visionary claim as well as the conviction that sharing stories is "one of the ways God forms us" give this lovely book its quality of humane hospitality. Readers may see in both observations a fair indication of what a pastoral heart its writer has brought to his work.

The generous appreciation for well-told stories we see in these pages is rooted in Doug's own respectful care for the stories of people he has served and loved. Good pastors listen deeply and well and sometimes help reweave torn lives into something new and beautiful for God. Introducing himself simply as "a pastor and a reader," Doug shows how, time after time, the stories we read and return to can enable us to see our own and each other's in new and gracious ways. They can help us be less quick to judge. They can help us develop the courage and will to see the suffering behind bad behavior and the beauty in quiet acts of neighborliness and the comedy in our inevitable misapprehensions of others' moods or motives.

It has been my privilege to read these chapters as they emerged during and after the months I worked with Doug's writing group in the doctor of ministry program where they began. His work in that program, designed especially for pastor-theologians who were also called to write, consisted not only of his own reading and reflection and refreshment of literary disciplines but also of his steady, quiet support of fellow pastor-writers. Most good writing is rooted in good conversation, and it was a pleasure to see good conversations emerge among seasoned, psychologically astute, self-aware adults with the humility it takes to be lifelong learners and the faith to say yes to developing their own skills. Doug was one of those clearest about wanting his hours of solitary work with words to serve his deepest purposes as a pastor.

Foreword

No stranger to the challenges that face local churches, nor to those that face families trying to navigate the confusions of contemporary culture, Doug has inscribed in these readings his own acute awareness of our common needs and our need to reclaim common ground as people of faith. I feel certain that you who read these chapters will find as you finish them that you have been ministered to, that you have experienced epiphanies and "shocks of recognition" along the way, and that you have been drawn into a wide circle of shared concern. Something of what binds us together as humans, neighbors, brothers and sisters, and pilgrims on this earthly journey will be newly apparent. I hope you settle in and enjoy this book and all the stories it invites you to revisit. Since a good book deserves more than one reading, I may just pick this one up again and do the same.

Marilyn McEntyre, author of *Caring for Words in a Culture of Lies*

Acknowledgments

WRITING A BOOK REQUIRES a lot of help. I have had a wonderful team.

These chapters began in the Sacred Art of Writing cohort at Western Theological Seminary (class of '24). Our guides, Winn Collier, Marilyn McEntyre, and John Blase, provided the perfect combination of instruction and inspiration. We all realized early on that we had stumbled upon something special. The friendships, giftings, and laughter during these three years created the environment I needed to attempt a book-length manuscript. Thank you all for sharing your writing with me.

Marilyn McEntyre was my English professor as an undergraduate at Westmont College. The opportunity, twenty years later, to reunite with her as my doctoral advisor and, effectively, my editor, was a kindness of God's providence I never expected. Her generous gift of time, encouragement, and gentle critique made this entire project better in every way. Her willingness to write the foreword is just one more example of her unending generosity.

Many of the ideas in these chapters started as conversations around tables full of delicious food with The Useless Pastors—Steve, Dan, Dan, Jeremy, Matt, Matt, and John. They have been my sounding board for ministry for fifteen years. Our annual gatherings are a joy.

Thank you to Darby Cavin, Scott Light, and Floyd Plemmons. Our post-Session sessions in the Bridges' "library" were foundational for helping me think through the life of a congregation.

Early readers included Finnlea Basler, Dan Baumgartner, Katlyn DeVries, Ian Doreian, John Leggett, Steve Lympus, Joan Mahaffey, Hudson Neeley, Chase Replogle, and Matt Royston. Thank you for your time, encouragement, and suggestions.

Special thanks to Ivy Bowers for the use of her painting, "Clear Cut" (oil on canvas), for the cover design. Ivy worked with me at First Presbyterian

Acknowledgments

Church of Aberdeen. God has always used artists and musicians to inspire and sustain me in ministry. Ivy's collection of work is as local as art can be and captures the glory, struggle, and hope of our Pacific Northwest town (she captures the rain too). It is an honor to have this stunning piece on the cover.

My mother, Glola Basler, was a reader. Books were everywhere in our childhood home. I am a reader because of her. She would have enjoyed reading this book.

And to my wife, Katie, and our kids—Addie, Jackson, and Isaac. Thank you for a life full of books and baseball and hiking and running and soccer and laughter and fishing and Jesus. It all swirls and weaves and stitches together so beautifully.

Introduction

SEVERAL WINTERS AGO, I read Wendell Berry's novel *The Memory of Old Jack*. I try to limit myself to only one of the Port William books each year. I do this, in part, because there is so much else out there to read, but also because I don't want to finish the series. I want Port William to be with me to the very end of the age. I realize this plan won't work forever. Berry is prolific, but he is also now in his nineties. At some point, I will catch him.

The Memory of Old Jack tells the story of Jack Beechum's final day through his regular loitering stops—the wood stove at Beriah's mercantile, Jayber Crow's (the barber) front porch, his sister's farmhouse for dinner, and the hotel-turned-nursing-home where he resides. At each stop, the story traces Jack's life, as the title indicates, through his memory. Young Jack Beechum was a man coming to terms with his ambition and limits. He succumbs to the idea that what he needs is more than his land can give. Here is how Berry describes it:

> What he had in his mind now as he sat and thought, or walked the lengths of afternoons and thought, or worked and thought, was more land. He wanted more land. A man falling in his own esteem needs more ground under his feet; to stand again he may need the whole world for a foothold. . . . Once he had hungered for the life his place could be made to yield. Now he would ask it to yield another place, at what expense to itself and to him he could not then have guessed.[1]

Jack's ambition comes at great cost. The sentence, "A man falling in his own esteem needs more ground under his feet; to stand again he may need the whole world for a foothold," is Berry at his best. One sentence captures the devastation of Jack's interior world. But the story is not without hope. Jack

---

1. Berry, *Memory of Old Jack*, 50.

Introduction

learns the gift of contentment. Contentment is humility. Humility does not come naturally to most of us.

I have been a pastor for twenty years. My own search for a foothold has landed on numbers and the ever-elusive definition of ministry "success." Instead of more land, I often believe more people in the pews will bring my salvation and peace. Even though practically and theologically I know that more people and peace never go together. In darker moments, it isn't just numbers but the notoriety that bigger numbers bring. In those moments, the people who have entrusted themselves to me become a means to my ambition and I fail them.

Jack was grasping for more. His story is not unique. When I read *The Memory of Old Jack*, I had already been reading Berry's essays and poetry for over a decade. I had known of my own grasping for at least that long. I didn't need Jack Beechum to teach me anything new. But like all good stories, Jack's story reawakened my own. It invited me back to sanity and health. It exposed the idols of my heart. It humbled me. It cast me, once again, upon the grace of Jesus.

I am a pastor and a reader. I believe God uses all of life to shape us into Christlikeness. Scripture reading, prayer, corporate worship and the Lord's Table keep us "in step with the Spirit" (Gal 5:25).[2] Over time, God's Spirit produces fruit in our lives like love and joy, peace and patience. The Spirit can also use parenting. Or gardening. Or reading. Not in the same exact way as the classic means of grace; a novel by Wendell Berry is not inspired like Paul's Letter to the Philippians. But I'm convinced that the habit of reading literature has shaped me as a follower of Jesus and has made me a more faithful pastor.

It's no secret that those of us who attend churches know that churches are struggling. Institutional dysfunction, cultural conflict, a glut of distractions, and everyday sins collude to erode our imagination for our life together in Jesus. I've found that reading literature, especially in community, can help shape a more hopeful vision of congregational life. One discipline we need, in our distracted age, is to sit and read a good story. An hour of reading develops a different set of muscles. It forces us to slow down. Haste is the enemy of growing. It keeps us from noticing what God is doing in us and through us and among us. Jesus calls us to a life of faith, hope, and

---

2. All Scripture references, unless otherwise noted, are taken from the New International Version.

Introduction

love. But faith isn't generic. We work out our faith in the details of our lives. You are not called to love people in the abstract. You may be called to love Steve, three doors down, who still has his campaign sign for the candidate you despise standing in his yard two years after the election is over. Reading fiction can help you with Steve. The Christian life happens in specifics.

The title, *All Swirling and Weaving*, is a phrase from Brian Doyle's novel *Mink River*. Doyle reminds us how stories thread a community together. He writes,

> And so many more stories, all changing by the minute, all swirling and braiding and weaving and spinning and stitching themselves one to another . . . so many stories braided and woven and interstitched and leading one to another like spider strands or synapses or creeks that you could listen patiently for a hundred years and never hardly catch more than shards and shreds of the incalculable ocean of stories just in this one town.[3]

Doyle's image of stories swirling and braiding and weaving together offers a way of imagining stories as part of the air we breathe—the atmosphere we create among us. Sharing them is one of the ways God forms us. God takes the "incalculable ocean of stories" that are happening all around us and stitches them together, often in ways we can't see or discern at the time. Reading has helped me to see how the stories of my own life and ministry have been woven together.

I wrote this book not only for pastors and ministry leaders, but also for readers who know the particular joy of walking into a bookstore. And for anyone who still aches for the life and health of Jesus's church. Each of the twelve chapters offers my reading of a novel as I reflect on how it touches my own life and faith. You don't need to be familiar with these novels, although I hope my reflections inspire you to read them. My prayer is that this book will encourage you to continue the slow, often unglamourous, process of learning to follow Jesus with the unique people and in the unique place God has called you.

I have found that reading with others, in small groups who pause and talk about what they found or loved or were puzzled by, opens understanding in ways that reading alone does not. Other readers' reflections begin to weave and swirl and stitch together. So let me end this introduction with a suggestion. One way to use this book would be to read the novels I chose with a small group of friends or church members and then read my

---

3. Doyle, *Mink River*, 13.

Introduction

reflections as an introduction to your own conversations. If your church doesn't have a book group, start one. Or ask a few friends to read with you and have them over for coffee to talk about it.

The novels I have chosen are a sampling of the books I read over the course of two years. Some were books on my to-read list or the latest novel by some of my favorite authors. *Mink River* showed up on my doorstep in an Amazon delivery bag without any name or hint of who sent it. I still do not know who gave it to me, but I am grateful they did. I intentionally include extended quotes from the novels to introduce you to the author's style and tone. I also include stories of my life as a pastor. I have changed names and situations as needed to try to honor the people I have had the privilege of serving and loving, and with whom and from whom I have learned so much. This book is dedicated to them.

On Reading and Pastoring

Claire Keegan's *Small Things like These*

Anyone serious about the distinctive conditions of the pastoral calling, story, person, place, will welcome these novelists as friends and spend time in their company.

Eugene Peterson, SUBVERSIVE SPIRITUALITY

EARLY IN MY PASTORAL ministry, I was invited to a cabin overlooking Useless Bay on the southern coast of Whidbey Island across Puget Sound from Seattle. The bay is stunning but too shallow for large ships to enter, hence the name, Useless. Steve, a friend of mine from when we served churches on opposite corners of Yellowstone National Park, had recently moved to the Tacoma area and had gathered a small group of pastors he knew for a three-day retreat.

Several of us had attended large conferences for pastors in the past with nationally known speakers. I found it a particular joy to sing with hundreds of other pastors at those events, and the keynote sessions were always inspiring, but they never seemed to connect to my experience in ministry. The speakers often served churches with staffs that were larger than my congregation.

Most of the pastors at Useless Bay were connected to a church on Queen Anne Hill in Seattle. Many of us were just getting started in ministry. Before we arrived on the island, Steve sent an itinerary for the retreat. At the top of the page, centered like a title, was the question, "What in the world are we doing? Conversations on Pastoring." It was a sparse schedule of focused conversations, eating, and free time to walk or run or read. We

All Swirling and Weaving

were also asked to finish a short novella called *Journey to the East* by Herman Hesse. Hesse was a German writer from the first half of the twentieth century; I had never heard of him.

It is now 2025 and that same group of pastors continues to get together every May. After a few years we stopped meeting on Whidbey Island because the cabin was no longer available, but we kept the moniker to name our annual retreat—The Useless Gathering. We refer to each other as the Useless Pastors. The itinerary still comes every February or March with more elaborate menus and the same loose schedule of conversations and walks in between meals. The title, "What in the world are we doing?" has remained. A lot has happened in eight different families and over twenty congregations in the past fifteen years. We are all married and most of our kids are now teenagers. There has been no shortage of pain and challenge at home and varying degrees of difficult congregational settings. But we are all still pastors. Statistically this is an anomaly.[1] The Useless Gathering marks the time. We laugh a lot—full-bodied laughter. Several of them are gifted musicians and so we sing. We hold each other's stories. They keep me going.

Thinking back to our first shared reading, I couldn't tell you what Hesse's *Journey to the East* was about. I remember feeling like I had missed some esoteric meaning to Hesse's novella and was anxious at that first gathering. Would I have anything clever to say? My fears quickly dissipated. I don't even know what we talked about, but I do remember the joy of having a conversation about a short story over a brunch of lemon-banana pancakes and peppered brown-sugar bacon with a table full of pastors. We are still reading together. Every year we read something prior to arrival. We have read novels, short stories, one-page articles, and extended essays. Most of the reading has not been directly related to ministry. I have noticed the length of reading has grown shorter every year.

The Useless Pastors are all men, we are all White, and we are all Presbyterian. Our congregations vary in size. Most of us are disciples of Eugene Peterson. Our experience is clearly not universal, but I also don't think that it is unique. My guess is that pastors of all ages, denominations, and theological commitments wonder the same thing we continue to ask each year: What exactly are we supposed to be doing? This question is not unique to being a pastor. This is a question relevant to all our lives. What exactly are any of us supposed to be doing as we learn to follow Jesus?

---

1. According to the Barna Group, in 2022, 42 percent of pastors were considering leaving the ministry. Barna, "Pastors Quitting Ministry," para. 2.

On Reading and Pastoring

I was floundering in my initial years of ministry when I first read Peterson's *Working the Angles*, his attempt to answer that same question. I was floundering because most of the metaphors offered for pastors and churches used language from the business and technology worlds. There were boards and committees—Buildings and Grounds, Finance, Christian Education—and monthly profit and loss spreadsheets from QuickBooks. Meetings with motions and seconds and Robert's Rules of Order. The how-to-be-a-pastor books were about vision and leadership, networking and adaptive change, family systems and conflict management. *Missional* was the buzzword of the time and with it came mission statements, vision statements, core values, and five-year plans. Some of this is necessary and helpful. But it didn't seem congruent with what we were trying to do as a congregation.

My first call was to a church in a town with only one hundred permanent residents. Having a flashy graphic for the next sermon series wasn't a top priority. I read the New Testament letters to the churches and the teachings and trajectory of Jesus's life, and our purpose seemed straightforward—the local church is a group of people learning to follow Jesus together. The conditions of our culture and our hearts make such following difficult. The trajectory of Jesus's life, from humble birth to twenty-seven years of obscurity to death on a cross, does not map well with the American dream. I needed a better metaphor.

Peterson wrote with a prophetic tone against the popular assumptions about pastoral leadership and church life. Instead of the pastor as CEO he suggested three pastoral "angles," like a triangle: prayer, reading Scripture, and spiritual direction. He kept using the word *personal*. Peterson assumed that if pastors were going to help members follow Jesus, they needed to know what was going on in the specific lives of their congregation. People don't follow Jesus in general, people follow Jesus in the details. Peterson's vision for the pastoral life resonated. But where did he find this alternative vision of ministry? Reading Peterson, it didn't take long to learn he wasn't reading pastor books either. He was reading novels.

Peterson was an expert in ancient languages and familiar with biblical scholarship, but he also read fiction and poetry. In fact, you get the impression that he read novels more than anything else. In several of his pastoral books, he tells the story of how he would put Dostoyevsky on his calendar two days a week to ensure that he had time to read. He knew his congregation might question using his paid time on *The Brothers Karamazov*, but nobody would argue if he simply told them he had an appointment on the calendar.

In an essay titled "On Novels and Pastors," Peterson explains his rationale for being a pastor-reader:

> *I am setting out vocational, not personal, reasons for pastors to read novels*, reasons that have to do with the kind of work we do and the conditions in which we do it. Pastors proclaim the story of God's salvation in Christ to specific people in a particular place. . . .
>
> Anyone serious about the distinctive conditions of the pastoral calling, *story, person, place*, will welcome these novelists as friends and spend time in their company.[2]

Peterson recognized that novelists care about people (their characters), places (their setting), and story (the plot). Pastors care about the same. Our lives are spent with unique people in specific places, and our primary calling is to proclaim the story of God and help others pay attention to how their stories connect to the Jesus story.

I would add *words* to Peterson's story, person, place. The best writers care about words. The best pastors care about the Word. And like novelists, we use words far more than anything else in our vocation.

While it took some time to connect reading fiction with my life as a pastor, there was a foundation laid in my childhood penchant for reading. *My Side of the Mountain*, *The Call of the Wild*, *Where the Red Fern Grows*, *Charlotte's Web*, and others were my constant companions. I owned a light-blue Fisher Price record player with a built-in speaker that played seven-inch vinyl records. My parents bought an abridged version of the BBC's audio edition of *The Hobbit* on record. I would listen to it over and over again as I fell asleep in elementary school. In college, I majored in English simply because I wanted to read good books.

Two years out of seminary I realized I hadn't read a novel in years. I read the Bible, commentaries, theology, and other nonfiction all the time. When our daughter, Addie, was just starting to talk I would often come home to have lunch with her and Katie. When I would head back to the church office, Addie would ask, "Are you going to look at your books?" I was surrounded by words, but I didn't make time for fiction. Reading Peterson's thoughts on the connections between pastors and novelists felt like an invitation to begin again.

---

2. Peterson, *Subversive Spirituality*, 186; my italics.

On Reading and Pastoring

I have never been disciplined enough in my time management to schedule regular hours for reading or put novelists on my weekly schedule. But for the past fifteen years I have always been working my way through a novel. It is difficult to quantify how this has shaped me as a pastor. I rarely reference or quote books in my sermons. I don't read attempting to psychologize or spiritualize characters for tips on pastoral care. A classmate of mine recently suggested that considering Artificial Intelligence, live streamed sermons, and online counseling, the pastoral role has become, more than ever, a commitment to "being a human amongst humans."[3] Novelists invite me to pay attention to the details of everyday life; they remind me of what makes us human.

This past May, the Useless Pastors read the short story *Small Things like These* by Irish writer Claire Keegan. Keegan manages to open up more of the world in a few sentences than most of us can in a thousand words. She introduces her story with words as crisp as the weather she is describing:

> In October there were yellow trees. Then the clocks went back the hour and the long November winds came in and blew, and stripped the trees bare. In the town of New Ross, chimneys threw out smoke which fell away and drifted off in hairy, long-drawn-out strings before dispersing along the quays, and soon the River Barrow, dark as stout, swelled up with rain.[4]

I have never been to New Ross nor seen the River Barrow. I had to look up the exact definition of a quay—the concrete or steel platforms alongside the water for unloading ships. But in three sentences we are firmly planted in a working-class town in the dreary days of early winter. November winds give way to December in New Ross and the local coal merchant, Bill Furlong, scrambles to deliver fuel to everyone in town before Christmas and before his overworked lorry fails to start.

The story takes a turn on the Sunday of Christmas week. Furlong finds a young girl locked in the coal shed at the local convent. His day started before dawn. Keegan's description of the scene outside his bedroom window foreshadows the depravity that is to come. "On the street, a dog was licking something from a tin can, pushing it noisily across the frozen pavement

---

3. Pastor Andy Stager used this phrase during a class conversation in the 2023 spring intensive of The Sacred Art of Writing cohort at Western Theological Seminary in Holland, Michigan.

4. Keegan, *Small Things*, 1.

with his nose. Already the crows were out, sidling along and letting out short, hoarse caws and longer, fluent kaaahs as though they found the world more or less objectionable."[5] The week prior, he encountered a few of the girls in the convent yard during a delivery. One of the girls asked him to take her down to the river so she could drown herself. The girl in the shed had been imprisoned longer than a night. She was freezing and famished and disoriented. She had a fourteen-week-old baby the nuns had taken from her.

Furlong wrestles with how to respond. He has five girls of his own. Their Christmas will be simple but warm and with laughter and cake. He was an orphan himself but managed a life because of the kindness of Mrs. Wilson, the woman who hired his mother as a domestic worker when she was sixteen and he was first born. Mrs. Wilson saw to his education and after he married, she helped him with a "few thousand pounds, to start up."[6] Her kindness inspires him and haunts him. The rumors of what went on behind the walls of the convent were well known. But there was little place for him to turn. He thought of taking the girl to the priests but "several times, already, his mind had gone on ahead, and met him there, and had concluded that the priests already knew."[7]

The entire story can be read in a short hour. Keegan gives voice to the women and lost babies of the Magdalene laundries of Ireland during the twentieth century. In her acknowledgments she notes that as many as thirty thousand girls may have been incarcerated and forced into labor in these convents "run and financed by the Catholic Church in concert with the Irish State."[8] It is a story about another unspeakable failure of the church. As well as the complicity of an entire town. And of the latent compassion emerging out of the depths of the local coal merchant. Near the end of the story, Furlong asks himself, "Was it possible to carry on along through all the years, the decades, through an entire life, without once being brave enough to go against what was there and yet call yourself a Christian, and face yourself in the mirror."[9] How can reading such a sentence not shape me as a pastor? As a person? Isn't this something of what we are supposed to be doing?

5. Keegan, *Small Things*, 54.
6. Keegan, *Small Things*, 8.
7. Keegan, *Small Things*, 110.
8. Keegan, *Small Things*, 116.
9. Keegan, *Small Things*, 113.

On Reading and Pastoring

I heard Russell Moore remark, "It is one thing to say, 'I believe in the forgiveness of sins.' And it is another thing to say, 'There was a man who had two sons.'"[10] What we declare in the Creed is true. I do believe in the forgiveness of sins. But Jesus knows how our hearts work. We need more than propositional truths. Jesus's story of the prodigal son and the waiting father in Luke 15 does something that the Creed, by itself, cannot do. It grips the imagination and the heart. Keegan's *Small Things like These* does the same. She shows the horrors of the Magdalene laundries and the inertia of indifference that allowed such horrors to continue in New Ross. The entire community is culpable to some degree. But she does this through the awakening conscience of Bill Furlong. My copy of Keegan's story is 116 pages. The young girl Furlong finds in the convent shed is not introduced until halfway through the book. The story is about him.

When I talked to friends about the book, however, I found myself claiming that the story is about the Magdalene laundry convents and the exploitation of poor women in Ireland during the twentieth century. My descriptions sounded like a news report—the number of girls, the fate of their children, the collusion of church and state. Those elements are in Keegan's story. But it is precisely because she doesn't tell it as a news report but in a story that her book has worked its way under my skin. It is likely the case that if I first heard of the Magdalene laundries scandal from a two-minute segment in the nightly news or as a hashtag on social media it would have just blended in with the rest of the noise of the day and been forgotten.

Fiction can do things that nonfiction can't. I still read thick tomes of theology. I even pick up a how-to-be-a-pastor book every now and then. But when it comes to learning the art of pastoring,[11] novelists have been my greatest allies. Fiction keeps me closer to our Useless Gathering question, What in the world are we doing? Somehow, though made up, novels keep me closer to real life. As Niall Williams says, "Books . . . are not life, can never be as full, rich, complex, surprising or beautiful, but the best of them can catch an echo of that, can turn you back to look out the window, go out the door aware that you've been enriched, that you have been in the company of something alive that has caused you to realize once again how

---

10. Moore, "Why We Need Fiction," 40:31.

11. To be fair, early in ministry I was greatly encouraged by a how-to-pastor book by David Hansen titled *The Art of Pastoring: Ministry Without All the Answers*. I am indebted to Hansen for the phrase "art of pastoring" and much more. As seen in the subtitle, his posture is different than most how-to books.

astonishing life is."[12] If being a pastor is learning how to be a human amongst other humans with Jesus, reading literature has helped me remember what it is to be human.

12. Williams, *This Is Happiness*, 73.

All Swirling and Braiding and Weaving and Spinning

Brian Doyle's *Mink River*[1]

Pied Beauty

Glory be to God for dappled things—
   For skies of couple-colour as a brinded cow;
      For rose-moles all in stipple upon trout that swim;
Fresh-firecoal chestnut-falls; finches' wings;
Landscape plotted and pieced—fold, fallow, and plough;
   And áll trádes, their gear and tackle and trim.

All things counter, original, spare, strange;
   Whatever is fickle, freckled (who knows how?)
      With swift, slow; sweet, sour; adazzle, dim;
He fathers-forth whose beauty is past change:
              Praise him.

GERARD MANLEY HOPKINS

    When my English professor read us "Pied Beauty" by Gerard Manley Hopkins, she warned us that she would not likely get through it. Her daughter has freckles. She made it through the "couple-colour" sky and the

---

[1]. An abridged version of this chapter was first published in *Ekstasis* (now Inkwell at Christianity Today) as "The Poetry of a Pastor," December 2023. It is used here by permission.

"rose-moles all in stipple upon trout that swim." But, sure enough, when she got to "Whatever is fickle, freckled (who knows how?)," she broke down. I thought I understood why. And maybe I did, at least to the extent that a twenty-year-old was capable of understanding.

My professor was often moved to tears as she read passages of poetry or prose out loud to our class. Her pauses were not for dramatic effect but because she would get choked up by the writing. One of my seminary professors would do the same as he moved from a discussion about Greek verbs to a reflection on the grandeur of God's grace. My pastor in Gloucester, Massachusetts, would need to stop mid-sentence during his sermon to collect himself as he fought back tears and, after regaining his composure, would apologize to the congregation with something like, "Sorry, don't be embarrassed, this is just what I do."

I loved this characteristic in all of them, partly because I, too, know what it is like to be overwhelmed with emotion in the midst of preaching. But also because I know their tears came from a well of gratitude. And genuine gratitude comes only when you understand the details of life as a gift, as grace.

The gift of Hopkins's poem is the surprise and freshness of his word choices. "Glory be to God for. . . ." You could end that sentence with any number of things, but "dappled things" comes as a surprise. It is fun to read the poem out loud. Try it.

> For skies of couple-colour as a brinded cow;
> For rose-moles all in stipple upon trout that swim;
> Fresh-firecoal chestnut-falls; finches' wings;

The variety of nouns and adjectives and sounds clearly come from someone who walks through the day slow enough to pay attention.

Like Hopkins, Brian Doyle was a poet who savored language. He also wrote essays and novels, but even in his prose he couldn't avoid being a poet. I read his first novel, *Mink River*, this winter. The novel is intended to show the confluence of the lives and events of the characters of a small coastal town in the Pacific Northwest. It is not a novel you read for the storyline. My sister-in-law told me she tried to listen to it as an audiobook on a road trip and quickly gave up. Like Hopkins's poetry, Doyle's prose invites to be read out loud but not as a page-turner. You want to savor each description, pause, and read them again.

Doyle introduces Mink River by claiming the town boasts nothing exceptional. It is "not an especially stunning town, stunningtownwise . . .

All Swirling and Braiding and Weaving and Spinning

but there are some odd sweet corners here."[2] He then introduces those odd sweet corners through the eyes of a soaring eagle:

> And down the street goes the eagle, heading west, his capacious shadow sliding like a blanket over the elementary school, where a slim older woman with brown and silver hair and brown and green eyes is holding court over the unruly sixth grade, her eyes flashing; . . .
>
> and over a lithe woman called No Horses in her studio crammed with carving tools as she is staring thoughtfully at a slab of oak twice as big as she is which isn't very big at all;
>
> and over a man named Owen Cooney who is humming in his shop crammed with automobile parts and assorted related ephemera as his pet crow sits quietly on an old Oregon State University football helmet watching; . . .
>
> and so many more stories, all changing by the minute, all swirling and braiding and weaving and spinning and stitching themselves one to another . . . so many stories braided and woven and interstitched and leading one to another like spider strands or synapses or creeks that you could listen patiently for a hundred years and never hardly catch more than shards and shreds of the incalculable ocean of stories just in this one town, not big, not small, bounded by four waters, in the hills, by the coast, end of May, first salmonberries *just* ripe. But you sure can *try* to catch a few, yes?[3]

What unfolds throughout the rest of the novel is Doyle's attempt to capture a few of the swirling stories, "braided and woven and interstitched," of the people and creatures of Mink River, Oregon.

As you can tell in the passage above, Doyle is not concerned with adhering to grammatical norms. Call me old fashioned but I like quotation marks and a sentence break every once in a while. Still, his frantic unraveling sentence structure offers us a way to see the world, the stories of the membership of Mink River all flow into and out of one another.

Doyle's story is filled with nouns. Entire paragraphs are sometimes just lists of things—"all trades, their gear and tackle and trim." The novel is a literary junk store of people, places, and things. Who doesn't love a book with a hand-drawn map in the opening pages like Tolkien's Middle-earth? The nouns are concrete and particular. It is not just a crow on a football

---

2. Doyle, *Mink River*, 11.
3. Doyle, *Mink River*, 12–13.

helmet in Owen Cooney's shop, it is a crow on "an old Oregon State University football helmet."

I am currently sitting in a Smoky Row coffee shop in the suburbs of Des Moines. On the table in front of me is my drip coffee in a for-here mug with a splash of 2 percent milk. My keys and phone and the camo duct tape billfold my kids made for me (fashionably decorated with yellow Minion stickers from the movie *Despicable Me*) are resting next to my black Moleskine notebook because I don't like sitting with stuff in my pockets. Eudora Welty's *One Writer's Beginnings* lies on top of the Moleskine. To the right of the laptop is my backpack, red and worn, chosen because it has a built-in rain cover for when I lived in Aberdeen, Washington, where it rains three hundred days of the year. The gray buckle on the sternum strap is missing a prong and so it no longer secures across my chest. My gray-and-black stocking hat sits slanted on the pack. We live in a tactile world, this is the gear and tackle of my trade.

One of Mink River's residents is a dying man. He is never named. Doyle first introduces us to him "as the man who has seventeen days to live."[4] He lives in hospice in the guestroom of the doctor's home. When he has only six days to live, he has a conversation with Danny, a boy injured in a bike accident, who is recovering at the doctor's house. He gives Danny a list of the objects he will miss as his life comes to an end. He says,

> These are the things that matter to me. The way hawks huddle their shoulders angrily against hissing snow. Wrens whirring in the bare bones of bushes in winter. The way swallows and swifts veer and whirl and swim and slice and carve and curve and swerve. The way that frozen dew outlines every blade of grass. Salmonberries thimbleberries cloudberries snow berries elderberries salalberries gooseberries. My children learning to read. My wife's voice velvet in my ear at night in the dark under the covers. Her hair in my nose as we slept curled like spoons. The sinuous pace of rivers and minks and cats. Rubber bands. Fresh bread with too much butter. My children's hands when they cup my face in their hands. Toys. Exuberance. Mowing the lawn. Tiny wrenches and screwdrivers. Tears of sorrow, which are the salt sea of the heart. . . .[5]

The list continues for an entire written page. It wanders from "the postman's grin" to "raccoons" to "cigar-scissors." The list concludes with, "My wife's

---

4. Doyle, *Mink River*, 121.
5. Doyle, *Mink River*, 195–96.

eyes, as blue and green and gray as the sea. The sea, as blue and green and gray as her eyes. Her eyes. Her."[6]

The list works. I have found myself picking up the book and rereading this list all week. But it is not because I share the dying man's affinity for furnaces or raccoons—no offense to either. It works because this is the stuff that makes up a life. You get the sense that this unnamed man with only six days to live has lived all of his previous days with wide-open eyes and a wide-open heart. Doyle's list invites me to pay attention to the things that matter to me. What would I include in a similar list?

These are the things that matter to me: The cold quiet mornings at Apgar campground. The taste of a hotdog cooked over a campfire. Letting my mind wander on a walk in the woods. The smile on Jackson's face when he hits a double. Mornings when Katie hits the snooze button on her phone and rolls over to rest her head on my shoulder; why do those nine minutes go by faster than any other? Reading out loud to the kids. Chopping garlic and onions. The beginning of a season, the beginning of a new book, the beginning of a semester. Syllabi. Wrigley Field. Addie's feet thundering on the hardwood in the kitchen when she first wakes up. Sunday mornings in the sanctuary before anyone else arrives. End-of-the-year book lists. The way the garden looks after weeding. Eating all the raspberries on the walk from the backyard before I get them into the house to rinse. Grandma Caswell's tomatoes. Sweet corn. Bookstores. Tomato pollen, the smell it leaves on my hands, my fingerprints yellowed after harvesting. Watching Isaac run, his smile while jogging back to the center line after a goal. Pat Hughes calling Cubs games on the radio.

Your list would no doubt be different from mine. Try it. But even though your list is different from the dying man's list in *Mink River* or my list above, I would guess some of the items are likely—laughably—familiar. The specific details of anyone's life often have a universal appeal. Gerard Manley Hopkins's poem "Pied Beauty" is, in one sense, simply a list of things that are spotted. Doyle's *Mink River* is a series of lists of objects and people and their happenings in a particular fictional town on the coast of Oregon over a period of a few months. Each, however, is brimming with life.

I started writing this chapter several weeks before Easter but as I was reading John's account of the resurrection this week in preparation for my Easter sermon, I was struck by the mundane details John chose to include.

---

6. Doyle, *Mink River*, 196.

All Swirling and Weaving

After Mary Magdalene finds the stone moved from the entrance to the tomb, John goes out of his way to mention three times that he beat Peter to the tomb as if it was some kind of foot race (John 20:4, 6, 8). He notes how the linen cloths used to wrap Jesus's body were on the ground in the tomb in three consecutive verses and how his head covering was neatly folded and placed by itself in the corner of the cave (20:5–7). It dawned on me that perhaps the first thing the risen Lord did after he defeated death, as his heart once again began to beat, was to fold his grave clothes. This seemed to me to be good news for laundry-doers everywhere—and especially to moms who probably still carry out the bulk of this mundane chore. The risen Christ folded his laundry. I suppose the angels could have done it, but angels probably don't have much experience with laundry.

John goes on to relate the moving encounter between Jesus and Mary in the garden after he and Peter leave. Mary is weeping. Weeping because she is grieving Jesus's death. Weeping because the Jesus movement that she had become a part of looked like it had come to a violent and sudden end on a Roman cross. Weeping because she could not even find Jesus's body. She keeps asking for Jesus's body. The angels in the tomb ask her about her tears. And then a man she mistakes as the groundskeeper, the gardener, asks her the same question. "Woman, why are you crying? Who is it you are looking for?" (John 20:15). Mary begins to leave in despair until she hears the man call her by name and she recognizes his voice. She turns and looks and sees Jesus, alive and well. She runs and embraces him. Her tears turn to joy.

Death had been defeated. The life and teaching and miracles and promises of Jesus had been fulfilled. Sin was judged and its power overthrown. New creation had begun. The final enemy had been conquered. But instead of dwelling on the cosmic realities of the resurrection, John tells the story of Easter by mentioning a foot race, folded grave clothes, and Mary's tears. The final chapter in John is just as ordinary. Jesus hosts a shore lunch with his disciples on the beach of the Sea of Galilee.

If Jesus really was alive that first Easter morning, and I believe he was, then all the stuff of life matters. The resurrection is God's "yes and amen" to life—not to some disembodied spiritual world of clouds and harps and angels in white but life on earth. Life we experience with our senses—taste and touch and smell and sight. Life with laundry that needs to be folded and fish fries with friends.

All Swirling and Braiding and Weaving and Spinning

Easter Mondays are hard. As a pastor I am worthless on Mondays in general but on Easter Mondays I feel most acutely the incongruity of what was declared the day before and the realities of everyday experience. The victorious declaration, "Christ is risen!" and then the response, "He is risen indeed!" starts our service. We sing resurrection songs and celebrate the promise of new creation. We hear about an empty tomb and Thomas touching the risen Lord's hand and side. We feast. And then Monday morning I have to drag the kids out of bed for school and pack yet another peanut butter and Nutella sandwich (PB&N is what our son Isaac calls them). The lawn needs to be cut and the edging done. And the unwashed Easter meal dishes sit on the counter taunting me. Christ is risen! Fold the laundry.

Reading *Mink River* and Doyle's lists of the objects and happenings of everyday life was a refreshing reminder of the real world Jesus came to rescue. It is the stuff of life that makes it life. Reminding the congregation of this is part of my job as a pastor.

A nun dies about a third of the way through the novel. In typical Doyle fashion, the description of this moment is both playful and profound. The nun's spirit floats up from her body upon her death but gets stuck on the broken ceiling fan where she overhears a conversation about her between the priest and the hotel manager. After both leave the room, Doyle writes,

> The old nun, or whatever she was now, had seen and heard all this, indeed she could see and hear far better than she could when she was alive, everything in the room now unbearably clear, everything its absolute self, everything rimmed with light like frozen dew rims twigs and leaves, the toaster shining, the refrigerator magnets shining, her coffee cup shining, the painting of Moses (the crow) shining, her to-do list with *fix fan!* on it shining, and she could hear for miles and miles, every sound crackling and distinct, every sound announcing its origin in a way she had never heard before. She heard owls, girls, trees, radios, fish, a fist landing hollowly on the chest of a boy, the suck of a baby at a breast. She heard a thousand thousand thousand sounds she had never heard before and would never have been able to identify before but now she knew them and loved them and had always known them and they were delicious and holy and necessary.[7]

The ridiculousness of the scene, a nun's ghost getting caught on a ceiling fan, is quickly overshadowed by the list of objects and sounds from the physical world. It is the sensual things—the things she can see and touch

7. Doyle, *Mink River*, 94–95.

and hear—that become shockingly vivid in her death. We were made physical beings and our great hope in Christ is that even after death we will one day, once again, have physical bodies and live in a physical place.

I officiated a funeral last week for a ninety-year-old man from our congregation. Dick was born into this same church. Six generations of his family have been baptized here. He taught mathematics and physics at a local university for thirty years. About twenty years ago, a man visited the church and Dick discovered that he had been treated poorly at a previous congregation. He needed friends and connection. So, Dick and a few other men from the church started a Wednesday morning coffee hour. And for two decades the same group of guys (adding some and losing others over time) have gathered week after week for two hours to drink Folgers coffee. The coffee isn't the reason they gather. They take turns buying donuts. They talk about anything and everything and nothing. Each has his own coffee mug. Dick's mug has the crest of the Urbandale Police Department and the D.A.R.E to Keep Kids off Drugs logo. Both are worn down so much that you have to look closely to make them out. These men know each other so well that long silences around the table are comforting, not awkward. They often work on minor projects around the church building. On Sunday mornings, the same group of men arrives an hour early and sits at the same table in the basement with the same coffee mugs, sipping Folgers before worship even though we have coffee hour after the service too.

The morning of Dick's funeral I went down to the church's kitchen and grabbed his mug. During the message I took the mug out from behind the pulpit and held it up for people to see as I described the wonder and the simplicity of the Wednesday coffee group. It was a large gathering at the funeral. I scanned the congregation and found the eyes of the men who had sat around that table week after week with Dick for so many years. Tears. Gratitude. It was just a coffee mug. It was only Folgers. But of course, it was more.

For many years, whenever I would read "Pied Beauty" my first thoughts would turn to my English professor's tears. Actually, for a while, my first thoughts were of spotted Yellowstone cutthroat trout, then to my English professor's tears. Then I had a freckled son of my own. Jackson is a wonder—compassionate and focused with a predisposition for justice. His thick, blond hair comes from Katie's dad and his smile from Katie, but he lives for sports as much as I did at his age. He reads great books and laughs with me at *The Princess Bride*. The world, and its stuff, is all before him.

All Swirling and Braiding and Weaving and Spinning

May God grant me a heart soft enough to always be a preacher who is moved to tears when I think of the gift that is captured in something as simple and perfect as the freckles on my son's face. Glory be to God for dappled things indeed.

Ruin Was Part of the Draw

Leif Enger's *Virgil Wander*[1]

For me...ruin was part of the draw.
Leif Enger, Virgil Wander

I was called to help revitalize a congregation that was closed to the public. It was a strange beginning. For the first four months, I was never in the same room with anyone from First Presbyterian Church of Des Moines because of the COVID-19 pandemic. I began by calling members, conducting meetings on Zoom, and preaching to my iPhone in an empty sanctuary, always wondering if anyone was on the other side.

My official title was Part-Time, Stated-Supply Pastor for Revitalization. I've never had business cards before, but that mouthful made it tempting to make some. By the time we were able to regather it became clear that the church would not survive. We had twenty active members.

We shifted focus from revitalization to faithfully closing the church after 174 years of ministry. Faithfully. I try to limit adverbs in my writing but this one matters. *Faithfully* closing. How do you celebrate and honor 174 years of ministry in a few months, give people time to grieve, try to connect the members to new congregations as if sixty years of relationships can just emerge, hold out hope that God is still at work in us and among us and through us, sell a big, old building with beautiful stained glass and a glorious sanctuary and bathrooms with missing tiles, disintegrating drapery,

---

1. An abridged version of this chapter was first published by *The Presbyterian Outlook* as "Closing a Church Faithfully," July/August 2023. Reprinted here by permission.

and toilets so old they probably use about a thousand gallons of water with each flush?

I baptized four-month-old Alys four months before we closed. The first person baptized in this congregation was baptized before the Civil War. We found handwritten minutes of elders' meetings from the 1870s. The decor of the building still held strong to the 1970s. I joked with my pastor friends that a decade ago I assumed I would be planting churches and now I am closing them. One friend suggested my new business card could read, Doug Basler, Church Killer: He's like Round-Up for your congregation.

While we were closing our church, I was reading Leif Enger's *Virgil Wander*. Rereading it, actually. I am an Enger fan. The midwestern storytelling and poetic prose of *Peace Like a River* rekindled my love for fiction in my early years as a pastor and I have anticipated Enger's subsequent novels, always wishing he would write faster.

The wonder of *Virgil Wander* is the community of characters. The story takes place in the fictitious Greenstone, Minnesota, on the shore of Lake Superior. Virgil is the narrator. He recently was released from the hospital after his "heartbroken Pontiac breached a safety barrier and made a long, lovely, some might say cinematic arc into the churning lake."[2] He was pulled out of the water by Marcus Jetty, a local scrap-store owner who was combing the beach for sellable junk. Virgil was left concussed but otherwise uninjured; his memory is slow to return and adjectives in particular prove elusive. Virgil's depleted vocabulary, however, is only a minor symptom compared to the more dramatic transformation his run-in with death produced. Virgil is a different man. He refers to his pre-crash self as the "Previous Tenant." He introduces his story with this:

> Now I think the picture was unspooling all along and I just failed to notice. The obvious really isn't so—at least it wasn't to me, a Midwestern male cruising at medium altitude, aspiring vaguely to decency, contributing to PBS, moderate in all things including romantic forays, and doing unto others more or less reciprocally.
> If I were to pinpoint when the world began reorganizing itself—that is, when my seeing of it began to shift—it would be the day a stranger named Rune blew into our bad luck town of Greenstone, Minnesota, like a spark from the boreal gloom.[3]

---

2. Enger, *Virgil Wander*, 3.
3. Enger, *Virgil Wander*, 3.

All Swirling and Weaving

The unspooling picture is Virgil's life. Virgil, a bachelor, owns the Empress Theater—an old-fashioned single-screen movie theater where he still does a live welcome before each night's showing. The Empress had not made money in years. Buckets were scattered all over the auditorium to catch leaks from the roof.

Virgil purchased the Empress Theater under the "doltish conviction that romance finally wins."[4] Even the previous owner did his best to try and talk him out of the deal.

> When I came to Greenstone as a grown orphan and failed theology student, the town was already past—the mines finished, the Slake plant padlocked. Kids would shout on Main Street and listen for the echo. The silent ore docks on their stilts had an impenetrable air, as though constructed by aliens or, why not, Egyptians.
>
> For me—as for Tom Beeman later, as for Alec and Nadine—ruin was part of the draw.
>
> In 1987 you could buy a house a block off the lake for nine thousand dollars, or a movie theater with an art deco marquee and catastrophic upholstery for thirty. I was fresh out of God but had adequate cash. I did both.[5]

Virgil's parents had died in a train wreck on a mission trip to Mexico when he was in high school. He briefly attended seminary but it didn't take and so he began a new life in Greenstone. He inherited a closet full of illegal reels of old films, some classics and some just old. The theater became a community haven. The pirated films became the catalyst for late-night watch parties where Virgil gathered friends for dinner and a movie. There was fellowship and community and laughter—the meals became potlucks reminiscent of our last gatherings in the Des Moines First Presbyterian Church's basement on Sunday afternoons.

Virgil's dilapidated Empress Theater reminded me of our church building. The office greeted you with the piercing stench of dog urine from a previous pastor's pets. Water damage had stained the walls in the basement and the woodwork in the ceiling of the fellowship hall. The main bathroom had half-inch clear tubing coming from a closet that emptied into a drain in the middle of the floor. You had to step over it to get to the toilet. Let's just say, the church growth movement would have a few recommendations on some upgrades. And rightly so; major work was

---

4. Enger, *Virgil Wander*, 95.
5. Enger, *Virgil Wander*, 93.

deferred for decades. Patches were patched and Comet with Bleach, the white powder in the green can ubiquitous to church janitor closets, was used liberally in an attempt to mask the smells. But there was more happening in the building than neglected repairs. Friendships were forged between unlikely acquaintances—Kathy and Midge, Molly and Steve, Gladys and Nate. Meals were shared. Prayers were prayed and answered. The gospel was read. A people gathered around a table and communed with the living God of the universe. Goats were purchased for families through Heifer International. Kids were sent to summer camp. Cancer and death and divorce were endured. Couples committed their lives to one another and their marriage to God. Elders and deacons were elected, ordained, and prayed over. Jesus was worshiped.

All of this could have happened at another location. These same types of things happen anywhere, everywhere, all the time. But it is hard to imagine any other place where this particular group of people would have gathered together for a common purpose. Eugene Peterson reminds us:

> The work of salvation is always local. Geography is as much a part of the gospel as theology. The creation of land and water, star and planet, tree and mountain, grass and flower provides ground and environment for the blessings of providence and the mysteries of salvation . . . nothing spiritual in our scripture is served up apart from material . . . this street, these trees, this humidity, these houses. Without reverence for the locale, obedience floats on the clouds of abstraction.[6]

I am writing this on a July afternoon in Des Moines, Iowa. I know "this humidity." My mom used to say these were the days on the farm when you needed gills more than lungs. One of our final major purchases as a congregation was a new air conditioner for the sanctuary because of "this humidity." Air conditioning wasn't an issue when I pastored in a coastal town in the pacific northwest (at least not yet). But we were in east Des Moines. It was on this water-stained linoleum tile and with these floral-patterned coffee mugs with jugs of powdered creamer that would never fully dissolve at 3100 Easton Boulevard where the life of Christ was formed in this congregation.

Bill picked up the church's mail every day from the hand painted mailbox at the entrance to the parking lot. He dropped off the mail in the office and made a walk through the building, checking for leaks or lights left on

---

6. Peterson, *Subversive Spirituality*, 190.

All Swirling and Weaving

by negligent staff (namely, me). He changed light bulbs, fixed toilets, ran the sound system, and maintained the furnace. He was the first one there on Sunday mornings and the last one to leave and always in a full suit.

The church building had an inaccessible courtyard off the front entrance. It was sunk down a full story below the main level of the building and was there for aesthetic reasons as far as I could tell. It housed a stone sundial that was donated to the church and some nondescript shrubs around the windows. Bill, who is in his eighties, would lower a push mower by rope down into the courtyard, climb down a fire-escape ladder and mow the small strip of grass and then hoist the mower back up again.

Imagine being told you can no longer go to a place that you returned to every day for decades, a place you returned to not because you had to, but because it was where you wanted to be. But now it is going to be closed, sold, and, depending on the buyer, it may be torn down and turned into an apartment complex or a storage facility. Bill's daily liturgy was as central to who he is as a human being as anything we would do on Sunday mornings.

The church needed to fold. Keeping it open so that Bill could continue to hoist his mower each week by rope would not have made sense. But it is hard to disconnect the faith, hope, and love being cultivated in his life from this place. Obedience and confession, generosity and sacrifice, laughter and mourning, service and the sharing of gifts all happened here.

I recognize, theologically, the church is a group of people and not a building. And in one sense, the space in which this group gathers is not critical. Churches can and have gathered in homes, in parks, in elaborate cathedrals, in open multipurpose rooms, in school auditoriums, and in YMCA gymnasiums. For much of my ministry I have gone out of my way to refer to our building as the *church building* and not simply as the *church*. I am sure the phrase "We don't go to church, we are the church" has come out of my mouth in one form or another dozens of times. But God meets people in particular spaces; ministry doesn't happen in nameless places.

In the Gospel narratives, Peter becomes a disciple while fishing on the Sea of Galilee. Peter was washing his net after a night at sea. They "worked hard all night and [hadn't] caught anything!" (Luke 5:5). Jesus gets in Peter's boat, takes him out into the lake and instructs him to cast his net. Peter was a fisherman. He knew when to fish and when not to fish. But he listens to Jesus, throws his net in the lake, and catches such a large number of fish that the nets begin to break. Peter sees the majesty of Jesus for the first time on the waters of Galilee and he drops everything to follow him. Later, while

Jesus was off praying on his own, the disciples began to sail across the sea in the middle of the night. As dawn approaches, Jesus walks to them on top of the water. The disciples are terrified. Peter said to Jesus, "Lord, if it's you, tell me to come to you on the water" (Matt 14:27). Jesus does and Peter walks, albeit briefly, on the waters of Galilee.

At the end of John's Gospel, Peter denies knowing Jesus three times, just hours before the crucifixion. The rooster crows and Peter runs away in shame. After Jesus's resurrection, Peter and some of the other disciples are back in the sea fishing. Again, they are not finding any fish. In the pre-dawn light of the morning, Jesus comes to the shoreline, but they do not recognize him at first. He calls out to the disciples, "Friends, haven't you any fish?" (John 21:5). Fishermen always love a question like that. Jesus instructs them to cast their net to the right side of the boat. They hauled in 153 fish and Peter realizes who it is on the beach. He dives into the water and swims to the resurrected Lord. After a breakfast of charbroiled fresh fish and bread Jesus asks Peter, "Do you love me more than these?" Peter responds, "Yes, Lord, you know I love you." And Jesus says to him, "Feed my lambs" (John 21:15). This happens two more times. Do you love me? Feed my lambs. Do you love me? Feed my lambs. Three denials. Three restorations. Peter is forgiven and recommissioned at the shoreline on the waters of Galilee.

Peter could have been introduced to Jesus anywhere. It could have happened in Capernaum at the market. It could have happened at a meal. It could have happened in a synagogue or in the town amphitheater or walking on the road. Jesus meets Zacchaeus in a tree and the paraplegic man on a mat lowered down from the roof. He meets the woman with a twelve-year flow of blood on a crowded street. Peter could have been a disciple even if the Sea of Galilee never existed. But it is hard to imagine that Peter ever looked at that lake without connecting it to the most significant moments of his life. It was in a fishing boat on *this* sea that he first decided to follow Jesus. It was on top of *these* waters that Peter took a few, literal, steps of faith. He experienced the indelible grace of Jesus's restoration on the shores of *this* lake after a fish breakfast with the risen Christ. I can't help but wonder what the apostle Peter would think if he heard that the Sea of Galilee was going to be drained and filled in to put in some condos and a Chick-fil-A? "The creation of land and water, star and planet, tree and mountain, grass and flower provides ground and environment for the blessings of providence and the mysteries of salvation."[7] It would be hard to separate Peter's faith from the Sea of Galilee.

In the same way it will be hard for Bill to separate his faith from his role as volunteer maintenance man for the First Presbyterian Church of Des Moines. Kathy can teach adult Sunday school for another congregation, but it will be in a different classroom than the one she has been in for the past decade. Nate and Andrea will find another nursery room in another church building to bring their daughters to when they need a break from sitting still in the sanctuary. But the nursery won't have the same Garden of Eden mural on the wall with Eve's hair and some tree branches strategically placed to cover hers and Adam's bodies. Or the same seven-foot stuffed animal boa constrictor for Gwyn to drag down the hall.

I am reading a journal by an Irish couple containing reflections of a year in their life maintaining their garden. The authors, Niall Williams and Christine Breen, purchased the house and land from her family over thirty years ago and raised their kids and worked the garden and scratched out a living through their writing. The area they live in was recently chosen as a suitable location for wind energy. Wind turbines were being installed less than five hundred meters from their home. But the winding countryside roads were not wide enough to bring the turbines in and so trees that have been part of the landscape for close to a century were ripped out and taken down before lunch one day. And the stone wall—made by hand with rocks found and placed presumably by some of Christine's ancestors over two centuries ago—that separates the road from the farms was plowed over. All for just one eight-hour workday when the delivery trucks would bring the over-sized turbine parts to the construction site. In the chapter I read this morning Williams writes, "Now it all gets taken in the mouth of the digger. Essentially, in our minds, what is going today is history, not in the abstract but in the most physical real way possible, in the actuality of the road itself and those who made it."[8]

As far as I can tell, Williams and Breen care about the environment. They love the land they are on and have cared for it for over three decades. They are in favor of wind and other "green" energies in general. But the impact this has on the real people living on these farms reminded me of how complicated everything truly is. The decision to put up wind turbines

---

7. Peterson, *Subversive Spirituality*, 190.
8. Williams and Breen, *In Kiltumper*, 196.

was done with good intentions. They have to go somewhere. But the turbines won't directly affect the people who made those decisions in the same way they will affect the people who will have to endure the twenty-four-hour swooshing noise a few hundred feet away from their heretofore quiet countryside homes. Those trees and that stone wall are gone. Listen to the way Williams describes losing the road he and Christine have walked most evenings for the past thirty-seven years:

> When you've walked the same road for more than thirty years it no longer has just a physical dimension. You're walking in memory and history; you're walking in the moment when on this same road you first let go of the back of the pink bicycle when your daughter sailed away from your hand and in fierce focus pedalled free for the first time. You're walking on the day you walked behind her in her wedding dress when she was sitting in a pony-and-trap that was being led by a top-hatted great-coated Tommy Ryan through the drizzling rain up to the Blessed Well for her to be married. You're pushing your son in a stroller whose best days are behind it and whose wheels never dreamed of a road this rough; it makes his head bob, but he likes it, and it's the same road he encourages you to jog along with him a quarter of a century later when it's your head bobbing and your bones jarring from the same roughness . . . it's the road you both walked with Huckleberry your dog for his fourteen years. It's the road you and Chris walked sometimes weeping, and sometimes without words, when she was trying to come through the chemotherapy.[9]

So, too, the church has far more than just a physical dimension. Singing "Be Still My Soul" on a blustery Sunday in February from the eighth pew on the left-hand side of the sanctuary might have been the place and the moment when the Holy Spirit started to put someone's life back together. How do you begin to quantify the significance of such a moment and such a place?

According to the statistical report of the Presbyterian Church (USA) there are currently 1,770 Presbyterian churches (20 percent of the denomination in 2022) with less than twenty-five members. A few years ago, my response to that number would have been, "Why do these places hold on for so long?" The statistics on churches that size becoming viable and healthy congregations again are extremely low. Maintaining those buildings alone often costs far more than the giving capacity of the congregations.

---

9. Williams and Breen, *In Kiltumper*, 49.

All Swirling and Weaving

Wouldn't the denomination be better served if those buildings were sold and the money used for missions and church planting? Wouldn't it make sense for some of those congregations to merge and join forces? Couldn't the buildings and land serve their communities in better ways? In many places the neighborhoods have changed dramatically, wouldn't it be better to have churches that resemble the new demographics of the neighborhood? I am sure the answer to these questions is still, "Yes, probably." I can't rationalize keeping them open from any practical or even missional perspective. The same could be said of Virgil Wander's Empress Theater. He sells only a handful of tickets each night.

And yet. Some account must be given to the reality that God has been at work in the lives of Bill and Kathy and Nate and Gwyn and Midge in this particular building. And God was at work in the lives of generations before them in the same place.

The congregation I served in Washington would often hold a twelve-hour prayer vigil on Good Friday. People would sign up for half-hour time slots from six in the morning until six at night. We would have a Good Friday service immediately following the vigil. Several years ago, my parents were visiting us during Easter weekend, and when we went to the church on Friday night my mom said she "loved to enter into a room that has been prayed in all day." I didn't understand what she meant exactly. The sanctuary looked as it had the day before when no one entered it to pray. The temperature was the same; the pews, the candles on the Lord's Table, the banners, the grand piano and organ, all were in the same spots; the giant large-print Bible sat on the table opened to the same passage in Isaiah it had been for weeks. But that day people had come and reckoned with God for thirty minutes and God, in turn, had reckoned with them. My mom could sense the difference.

I am not sure what account must be given. By the time anyone reads this, First Presbyterian Church of Des Moines will no longer exist as a congregation. The building will have been sold and either used by a new congregation or demolished to use the space for other purposes. Nostalgia is always a danger, a wistful longing for a past that was never truly the reality we imagine it now. I also am aware of the danger of the idolatry of buildings. Plenty of twelve-step groups have been denied access to church buildings because the hearts of the board couldn't see beyond coffee stains on the carpets and cigarette butts in the parking lot. Abuses of all kinds have happened in church buildings. A place that was light and life for one individual may have only been darkness and death for another.

Virgil Wander ends with some semblance of hope. The Empress Theater is given a new roof. A few businesses in Greenstone begin to prosper. Virgil gets the girl. But like most rural towns in America, its future is unknown and its past mostly vacated or bulldozed away. I trust the members of First Presbyterian Church have a brighter future than that. God has begun a good work in them and will carry it on to the day of Christ (Philippians 1:6). I had the privilege of witnessing the fruit of that good work and attempting to steward it as the congregation's last pastor. It is, nonetheless, sad that the place where much of that good work began will no longer be.

A Hundred Books Could Not Capture a Single Village

Niall Williams's *This Is Happiness*

One of the privileges of living in a place forgotten is the preservation of individuality.

Niall Williams, THIS IS HAPPINESS

"IT HAD STOPPED RAINING."[1] This is the opening sentence to Niall Williams's novel *This Is Happiness*. Three hundred and eighty pages later the story concludes, "It had started raining."[2]

In the dry spell between these rains, a generous tale unfolds of a summer in the village of Faha, Ireland. The setting is the government's installation of an electrical grid in rural Ireland in the late 1950s. It is a story about a man who organizes his life around the hope that he can make amends for a lifetime of bad decisions. It is a story of a lonely seminary dropout finding a friend after he has lost his faith. It is a story of two men on one bike, pub-crawling the Irish countryside in search of the elusive fiddler Junior Crehan. It is a story of a community resisting technological progress, aware of the diminished humanity it will bring. It is a love story with no frills or fireworks. It is a story that reminds us why we read books.

Faha is a place slightly off the grid. Noe Crowe, the narrator, describes it with this:

1. Williams, *Happiness*, 1.
2. Williams, *Happiness*, 380.

A Hundred Books Could Not Capture a Single Village

> A hundred books could not capture a single village. That's not a denigration, that's a testament. Faha was no more nor less than any other place. If you could find it, you'd be on your way somewhere else. The country is filled with places of more blatant beauty. Good luck to them. Faha doesn't care. It's long since accepted that by dint of personality and geography its destiny was to be a place passed over, and gently, wholly forgotten.[3]

Williams details this "dint of personality and geography" in ways both touching and humorous. I regularly laughed out loud while reading, which always makes my dog nervous. Electricity didn't arrive in parts of rural Ireland until 1977. For Faha it came in 1958, a year when 80 percent of homes in America already had a television set. That was the summer Noe went to live with his grandparents after his mother's death and after he dropped out of seminary. It also happened to be the summer that Christy McMahon rented a room from Noe's grandparents to work on the electrical lines and to try and right a wrong he had committed a lifetime ago. An unexpected friendship between the grieving Noe and the repentant Christy drives the narrative. Christy hopes to receive forgiveness from the woman he left at the wedding altar fifty years earlier. Noe is not exactly sure what he is searching for, but he finds comfort in his grandparents' hometown.

One of the many pleasures of the story is meeting the members of Faha. Looking back, Noe says, "In Faha, because the centre was distant and largely unknown, eccentric was the norm." He introduces us to the town membership by describing their seating arrangement at the parish church:

> Like those in the Ark, there was an unwritten order to how the parishioners came into St. Cecelia's and where they sat. Because they were the same people who came each week, strangers and foreigners being then virtually unknown, you could close your eyes and know that Matthew Leary, first in and last out, was prostrate in the front pew, pate lowered, prayer-hands clasped out in front of him, the weight of his sins imponderable and awesome; that Mick Madigan didn't enter but for reasons unknown stood just outside the church doors in the rain; that though she had come that morning from a house you'd see in a famine museum the small upright pillar of Mary Falsey was at the very front of the Women's Aisle, her husband Pat sniffling with permanent head cold at the back of the Men's.[4]

3. Williams, *Happiness*, 4.
4. Williams, *Happiness*, 7.

All Swirling and Weaving

I am drawn to Faha as I am drawn to Wendell Berry's Port William. The characters and their eccentricities are made up. But they're not, of course, in all the ways that matter. I would guess you, too, know someone who has a permanent head cold and sniffles through the winter. If you belong to a church community, you probably have a Matthew Leary and a Mick Madigan in your congregation; or you are a version of them yourself.

After seminary my wife, Katie, and I moved to a town of one hundred permanent residents on the edge of Yellowstone National Park for a three-year assignment. I was the town pastor; the next closest church was over sixty miles away. My side hustle was working as assistant supervisor of the town dump and as a waiter at the Beartooth Cafe. Katie managed the front desk of the Alpine Motel and taught at the one-room schoolhouse. She served as the substitute postmaster and waited tables on the side. This jumble of jobs meant we had as much access to the community as just about anyone. Most of its members, however, had no desire to be accessible.

At seven thousand feet, natural splendor was everywhere. It was why we were there. Our cabin and church building sat under the shadow of Mount Republic; our backyard was locally known as Moose Meadow. The few lifelong residents were surrounded by transplants who visited, fell in love with the place, and bought businesses to try to find a way to stay. The town had no law enforcement. The only way out by car during the winter was a sixty-mile trek over snow-packed roads through Yellowstone. The state of Montana doesn't plow the fifteen miles east of town to the Wyoming border, so more than a handful of church members came to Sunday worship by snowmobile. The yearlong residents had landed there to escape. Some, no doubt, were escaping their past or people they wanted to forget; but most were escaping disillusionment with the American dream.

After Barb and her husband sold their restaurant, she continued to bake pies daily for the Soda Butte Lodge. People came back every summer for the mountains, trout streams, and a piece of Barb's key lime pie. She even baked one for President Clinton when he passed through town to sign the New World Mine Property Agreement, which stopped gold mining in the area. Barb sang in the choir and was a regular at every church event.

Denny was a big-machine operator. He was not thrilled about Clinton's executive order. He sported a Santa Claus beard (and belly) and Carhartt coveralls all year long. He sang bass in the church choir and insisted we include "Still, Still, Still" every Christmas Eve. He lived with a Dalmatian named Snoopy and painted her toenails pink.

A Hundred Books Could Not Capture a Single Village

The talent concentrated in that community was impressive. For the first six months we lived there, Dan, our church's multi-instrumentalist, squatted on National Forest land a mile from town in his own makeshift camp. He hiked to work every day and back again every night. Not only could he play a dozen instruments, but he could also have managed the kitchen in a five-star restaurant anywhere in America. Dan took Wednesdays off so he could cook for our Bible study.

Kevin has published several books. He wrote in the mornings in a booth at Hoosiers Bar. At night he washed dishes at the Beartooth Cafe. In the afternoons, he casted for Yellowstone cutthroat in Soda Butte Creek.

Nate, a renowned nature photographer who had worked with the BBC, lived a half mile down the road from us. In the three years we lived there, I never met him. One of his photos, a silhouette of a moose in the moonlight, still hangs in our hallway.

The members of Cooke City, Montana were not simply an interesting cast of characters. They were the people we fished with in the summer and skied with in the winter. They were the people we complained with in the back of the kitchen about the annoying kids at table five. They took us snowmobiling in waist-deep powder. Their passions became our passions. And they were the people with whom we cried the afternoon Pat and Steve were killed in the jeep accident in the mountains above town. That morning, we had climbed ten-thousand-foot Mount Republic with Chuck Sumner. Mary Dye waited for us at the trailhead for hours to break the news. I was twenty-seven years old. An entire community was reeling. I had no idea how to comfort them; but I knew enough to try and point them to the God who could.

God used this community to teach me how to be a pastor. They were patient and generous and always encouraging. In his kindness, God, in turn, used Katie and me to encourage and love them back.

When I was in seminary, I took a course on the Greek exegesis of Romans. As in most classes, we were only a quarter through the syllabus by the time we were three-fourths finished with the semester. We examined Paul's intricate argument for grace in the first seven chapters. We marveled at the pinnacle of his theology in chapter 8. And we wrestled through some of the interpretive challenges of chapters 9–11. But after twenty years of pastoral ministry, my favorite section of Romans is the first half of chapter 16. We didn't even cover that chapter in class. It is a list of people Paul wanted to send greetings to. He mentions Priscilla and Aquila, Andronicus and Junia, Ampliatus, Urbanus and Narcissus (I imagine he was teased as a kid). He lists twenty-nine people in total—about the size of our winter congregation in Cooke City. In verse 13, Paul says, "Greet Rufus, chosen in the Lord, and his mother, who has been a mother to me, too." I take delight in the fact that Rufus and his mom made it into holy Scripture. Somewhere in his travels, Paul probably sat down with them over wine and fish and laughed at their stories. Maybe Rufus's mother made Paul broth when he was sick, or the first-century version of a key lime pie on his birthday. I appreciate theology as much as any Presbyterian, but it is this list of names at the end of Paul's letter that makes the most sense to me.

God is at work in the idiosyncrasies of life. Not life in general. No generic ministry exists. Jesus was at work in the string of events that made up Urbanus's life, and Junia's, and Andronicus's. He was also at work in the way those lives intersected in the worship and fellowship of the early church in Rome, including the arrival of this letter from Paul. Jesus doesn't just comfort in general; Jesus comforts Rufus during the particular challenges, losses, sins, and sufferings he experienced. It appears Jesus also used Rufus's mom to comfort Paul. Eugene Peterson said that one of his primary roles as a pastor was to introduce the word *God* into the events of his parishioners' lives—the extraordinary events, for sure, but, more importantly, the mundane ones.

Last night we were awakened by two kids with stomach flu. I "slept" the rest of the night on the couch in the basement next to our son Jackson and his blue two-gallon bucket positioned and ready. Katie did the same on the couch upstairs with our daughter, Addie. After their stomachs finally settled this morning, I went to the tire shop to have a flat tire repaired. The nail I ran over somewhere this weekend was too close to the edge of the tire to be patched, so we needed to replace it, which automatically meant we needed to replace two tires. By the time the new tires were installed, and I stopped at the store for some applesauce and Gatorade, I had to pick up our son Isaac from school. The day I had scheduled in my head last night was gone before it even started.

I doubt God intends for me to interpret too much in today's events. I am certain, however, that God is using a lifetime of days like today, and the ones with less vomit and more laughter, to instill within me more patience, grace, selflessness, and trust.

Reading *This Is Happiness* has the effect of slowing life down. It inspires an afternoon walk and a cup of tea to warm up, and a game of Dutch

Blitz after dinner with the kids. Slowing down enables us to pay attention. Paying attention is the only way to see that the world truly is "charged with the grandeur of God.[5]"

What makes Faha so compelling is precisely what the looming installation of the electrical grid threatens—conversation and a game of Forty-Five in the garden with Ganga, the Sunday gathering at St. Cecilia's and the high holy days that mark village time, and evening bike rides to the local pub. It is the pace and rhythm of the village that brings comfort to Noe in his grief. Looking back, Noe tries to describe the impact of the change:

> I am aware here that it may be hard to imagine the enormity of this moment, the threshold that once crossed would leave behind a world that had endured for centuries, and that this moment was only sixty years ago. Consider this: when the electricity did finally come, it was discovered that the 100-watt bulb was too bright for Faha. The instant garishness was too shocking. Dust and cobwebs were discovered to have been thickening on every surface since the sixteenth century. Reality was appalling. It turned out Siney Dunne's fine head of hair was a wig, not even close in colour to the scruff of his neck, Mick King was an out-and-out and fairly unsubtle cheater at Forty-Five, and Marian McGlynn's healthy allure was in fact a cake make-up the colour of red turf ash.[6]

The impact of electricity would be more significant than light bright enough to see Siney Dunne's wig. The way the villagers cooked, cleaned, worked, dried their laundry, entertained themselves, and ultimately gathered and interacted with one another would be changed and irretrievable. Along with the electricity, the world would come to Faha, and the uniqueness of the village would begin to fade. Life would speed up. And speed obscures detail. If you have ever walked a route in a town that you had only previously traveled by car you know what I mean. When you walk you notice cracks in sidewalks, the dead lower limbs of trees in the yards, the heavy red door on the house on the corner.

My job as a pastor is to learn the idiosyncrasies of the members of our congregation. What makes them tick? How do they put their world together? And that takes time, both in leisure and intentionality. Why does Kathy never come to church potlucks, but is always in the kitchen serving at the Feed the Hungry program? Pat is one of the strongest people I have

---

5. Hopkins, *Major Works*, 128.
6. Williams, *Happiness*, 53.

ever met; why does she weep every time we sing "The Power of the Cross?" Why do Don and Sherrie slip out of the sanctuary and into the parking lot during the closing hymn?

Clearly, Williams knows the answers to these types of questions about the characters in his novel. If a novelist knows his fictional characters with this level of precision, shouldn't a pastor take aim at knowing the congregation with the same depth? We are calling people to a life of faith, hope, and love. But apart from the actual details of a real person's life these remain just church words. They sound nice but quickly fade into abstraction.

Jason is not called to love in general; he is called to love his patients, who also happen to be prisoners in the state penitentiary where he serves as a physician's assistant. And he is called to love his nurses and staff along the way. Kevin is not called to hope as a dislocated concept but as the means of enduring, with the support of a few close friends who meet with him every Wednesday morning for breakfast, a decade of walking with his adult son through the rollercoaster of addiction. The gospel comes alive in the nuances of a person's weekly routines. Otherwise, it remains merely a list of propositions. My job as a pastor is to learn those personal nuances as deeply as I know the gospel's propositions.

In the acknowledgments, Williams says he wrote *This Is Happiness* in the company of "the extraordinary music of The Gloaming in Kiltumper."[7] I am writing this chapter in the same company, though I'm in Urbandale, Iowa. Their music *is* extraordinary. Still, I am sure it does not have the same effect on me as it does on those native to County Clare. Many of their lyrics are in traditional Irish. The best music, like the characters in this novel, is often rooted in a place. My favorite musicians are the ones you have never heard of—Jeff Menuey playing at Miner's Saloon in Cooke City; we all felt we were in on the same secret every time his band played "Montana Winter." Mattaniah and Ericka Corban singing on the lawn of Lake Quinault Lodge while our kids played homerun derby with the wiffle ball. John and Leslie O'Brien and Nick Greeley playing in the O'Briens' living room, the cello singing out, carrying us heavenward.

When Noe hears Christy singing at Craven's Pub for the first time "with screwed-up eyes and fists by his side a ballad about love," he makes this remark about art in general:

> It seems to me the quality that makes any book, music, painting worthwhile is life, just that. Books, music, painting are not life, can

7. Williams, *Happiness*, 381.

never be as full, rich, complex, surprising or beautiful, but the best of them can catch an echo of that, can turn you back to look out the window, go out the door aware that you've been enriched, that you have been in the company of something alive that has caused you to realize once again how astonishing life is, and you leave the book, gallery or concert hall with that illumination, which feels I'm going to say holy, by which I mean human raptness.[8]

    This Is Happiness catches such echoes. Williams's prose is alive with astonishment.

    We recently relocated to Des Moines, Iowa, after twelve years in rural Washington. We are finding the suburbs as disjointed as the stereotypes warn as we worship, play, work, and live in different communities. But we are surrounded by people. God's image is all around us. Most days it is exhausting to imagine getting to know any of them. Reading *This Is Happiness* reminded me of why it is worth it. There will one day, by God's grace, be new friends who regularly sit around our dinner table. And their passions will become our passions and ours theirs. And their sorrow our sorrow. And we will try to introduce the word *God* into the spaces of their lives where he hasn't been considered yet. And, hopefully, some of them will make music.

---

8. Williams, *Happiness*, 73.

The Membership
Wendell Berry's *Nathan Coulter*

It is those we live with and love and should know who elude us.
Norman Maclean, A RIVER RUNS THROUGH IT

NEAR THE CONCLUSION OF Wendell Berry's novel *Nathan Coulter*, Nathan, Brother (Tom), and their grandparents are eating breakfast in the kitchen. Late summer rains had led to frustrating farm work and humidity had left the window jambs swollen. It is a hot Kentucky morning and Grandpa asks Brother to get up and open the window. He fusses with it until Grandma comes over and tries to help; neither can get it to budge.

Grandpa removes his cane from the back of his chair and smashes the panes of the window. Nobody speaks. Brother sits back down. Grandma goes to the stove to take biscuits out of the oven. Grandpa turns around and finishes eating his breakfast, then heads out to the barn. Nathan, the narrator, tells us, "We ate without talking or looking at each other."[1] The silence is broken only when Uncle Burley sees the shattered window and begins to laugh.

It is a difficult scene in a story full of them. A window stuck by humidity is a minor inconvenience. Grandpa smashing out the kitchen window has a backstory. Nathan and Brother are living with their grandparents because their mother died and their father, Jarrat, in his grief, is unable to care for them. Burley, Nathan's uncle, has always been a disappointment to Grandpa and a constant worry for Grandma but remains under the same

---

1. Berry, *Nathan Coulter*, 71.

roof. Jarrat's barn just recently burned to the ground. Grandpa's body is breaking down and farm work is all he knows. In a world overgrown with thorns and thistles, a sticky window is the one thing, after all the others, that Grandpa can no longer bear.

Nathan Coulter is a story of death and frustration. Awkward silences serve as the soundtrack. It begins with the death of Nathan's mother and ends with Grandpa dead in Nathan's arms. Between those great losses everything seems to end in loss. Even promising moments like the 4th of July fair or Burley's and Nathan's giant catfish catch fizzle out in unmet expectations. Graveyards feature regularly in the narrative.

Conversations are stilted. Grandpa doesn't know what to say or to whom to say it; smashing the window is his way of communicating in the moment. Burley deflects his parents' frustration with laughter. When he's had enough, he retreats to the fishing shack down by the river. The only extended conversation between Jarrat and his sons is when he provokes them during the tobacco harvest into a competition that ends with a fist fight, after which Tom moves out. Tom outgrows Nathan, as older brothers do. Nathan recognizes that turning point when he stops calling him Brother and begins to refer to him as Tom.

Those familiar with the other Port William books know that at this point World War II is looming and Tom, along with numbers of other young men from town, will go off to war and not come back. Nathan doesn't have much time to renew his relationship with his brother. Grandpa and Burley remind us that even with time and proximity, reconciliation is not a given.

My aunt died last week. Aunt Sally in Pittsburgh. Growing up she was referred to only in connection with her husband, Uncle Roy. It was always "Aunt Sally and Uncle Roy," as if the two really were one flesh. I can count on one hand the number of times I was with her in person. She was my dad's only sibling. We lived in Chicago; they lived in Pittsburgh. Neither family went out of their way to visit. She was faithful in sending birthday cards. Even into my mid-thirties, married and with children of my own, I would receive a card each year with a crisp $5 bill and only her signature, "Uncle Roy and Aunt Sally."

I am unaware of any fissure in their relationship that would have caused my dad and my aunt to avoid each other. They talked regularly on the phone. But Aunt Sally and Uncle Roy were not a part of our lives. My parents were raising four kids in the Chicago suburbs with salaries from a church preschool and a small Christian college, so our travel was limited to holiday visits to Iowa to see my mom's side of the family. It didn't occur to me as a kid that I rarely saw the Pittsburgh family, including my grandparents. As an adult, I chalked it up to the reality that my parents were simply living their life and ministry in Chicago and that was complicated enough.

I helped my dad call Uncle Roy this morning to express our condolences and get details on the service. Aunt Sally had Alzheimer's, like my dad. Roy kept her at home as long as he could. He visited her in the nursing home every afternoon. He endured four hours of dialysis three days a week to care for his wife and see her through the end. I had no idea. As I listened to him speak with grace and candor and humor about Aunt Sally's last days and my dad's lucid, tear-filled gratitude for Roy's vigilance, I realized that not knowing this man, or my aunt, was a great loss for me.

A greater loss is the realization that much of my dad's life is now out of reach. At dinner I asked him to tell us about growing up in Pittsburgh. He cobbled together a broad picture about the misery of the Steelers and the Pirates and his own father's work as an engineer. He remembers the soot from the mills collecting on the windowsills and summers at the family cottage on Lake Eerie. But I don't know what he did with his afternoons after school, or the color of his house, or if he was picked on in high school, or if he did the picking. He has never shared what faith looked like in his family or when he felt called to become a pastor or how that call transitioned into higher education. I know my mom never felt she could meet the high standards of her mother-in-law, but I cannot remember my dad ever saying anything about his mom. How is that possible? And why did it never occur to me to ask before now?

Wendell Berry refers to the people populating his fictional town of Port William as "The Membership." It is a delightful designation. But *Nathan Coulter* reminds us it is not the idyll for which Berry's books so often leave us longing. Hardship imbues the Coulter's kitchen and settles in as a fog around the hearth of Beriah's general store; a suffering felt, even acknowledged, but only through silence. Jarrat owns the farm adjacent to his parents. His sons live in the house he grew up in, visible from his own. But he lives alone even in their presence. Port William offers an integrated life. The same neighbors who help with the tobacco harvest are the ones who meet for town gossip at the general store and the same ones who pass the bottle of moonshine around the circle at Burley's fishing cabin. But a distance remains amidst the familiarity.

The Membership

I have served in three congregations. The largest had a membership of about seventy-five people. I am convinced I can only care for people I know and who, in turn, know me. I easily critique large congregations, multi-site ministries, and pastors who have never met their members. But accessible size and proximity is no guarantee of intimacy. I remember a few years ago reading a one-page article titled, "Sometimes Small Is Just Small."[2] It resonated as I thought of members of our congregation who have worshiped side by side for decades, served on committees and volunteered to teach Sunday school together but have never been in each other's homes. They have never shared with one another the challenge of parenting a teenage daughter or the ever-growing distance between their expectations and how life has actually turned out.

The home and the local congregation should be the safest and easiest spaces to know others and to be known. Often, however, they can be the places in which we build the thickest walls. Maybe it is because the people we care the most about are also the ones we want to care for us, and therefore the ones from whom we most fear rejection. And while it is true that many homes and many congregations are not safe places, Lord have mercy, it is equally true that our fears are often unwarranted. If you have ever been in a small group long enough, I am guessing you have found that the group can go months, maybe years, hovering on the surface. Then someone finally finds the courage, or the desperation, to open up and share something meaningful. Defenses come down. "I'm not the only one" moments build camaraderie and strength; tears flow and prayers are offered. Healing happens. As Mike Emlet says, "Transparency begets transparency."[3]

In the fourth chapter of John's Gospel, Jesus has a conversation with a Samaritan woman at the well outside of her town. Jesus asks the woman if she would draw him some water. She is surprised by this and questions the propriety of their interaction. Jesus doesn't directly answer her but instead takes the conversation in a new direction. He tells her that if she knew who it was that she was talking to she would be asking him for "living water." She doesn't understand his reply and notes that since he has nothing to draw water with, how could he offer her anything? The back and forth continues and the woman's desire grows for this "living water" that would leave her satisfied forever. Then, Jesus reveals that he knows all about this woman. He knows she is not married but that she has had five husbands already.

---

2. I have not been able to locate this article, and I do not remember its source.
3. Emlet, "Fully Known," para. 9.

And yet he continues to engage with her. Her painful past, about which we are not given details, does not scare him away. She is seen and known and still accepted. At the end of the conversation, John tells us, she goes back into the village and invites the whole town to meet Jesus: "Come see a man who told me everything I ever did. Could this be the Messiah?" (John 4:29).

Is this not what we want from our communities and our families—to be known and understood and still loved? Why does such safety seem so out of reach? A friend of mine recently mentioned that he regularly invites his congregation to enter every encounter by remembering that the person they are talking to is a human being with a God-given desire for purpose, understanding, and connection. Even if they don't know it. I doubt Grandpa in *Nathan Coulter* would phrase it that way. But the need is there, nonetheless. Why does this level of care for one another so often seem unsustainable?

One poignant moment in *Nathan Coulter* is a scene on the day Nathan's mother died. Nathan's father, Jarrat, goes out to the woodpile in the yard and begins chopping. The undertaker takes her body and neighbors begin coming to pay their respects. They all watch Jarrat chopping wood from the back porch, focusing his grief into each swing. Nobody goes out to him. Berry writes,

> Grandpa came, riding his mare into the lot, and stopped on the other side of the woodpile. He looked at Daddy for a minute, as if he wanted to tell him to quit or say something to comfort him. He looked away finally and sat still, only jerking the bridle reins a little when the mare got restless and began to paw and toss her head. Daddy never looked up from his work. The axe blade glinted in the sun and came down. Grandpa spoke to the mare and rode home again.[4]

Grandpa's compassion leads him to stop. The weight of the moment is acknowledged and felt, and it's crushing. But he fails to speak. Grandpa talks to the mare but not to his grieving son. One word, even a hand to a shoulder, might have been enough.

Yet a resilience remains in Port William. Fidelity is what Berry would call it. Grandma and Grandpa don't understand Nathan's uncle Burley and Burley refuses to conform. But he remains. He is there at each planting and at each harvest. He is there to be a father to Nathan and Tom when Jarrat is unable to be, paralyzed in his grief. He is there to pass the bottle

---

4. Berry, *Nathan Coulter*, 27.

with the other lonely men from town at the fishing shack. Burley remains misunderstood, kept at arm's length, and yet loved. And he, in turn, loves those who don't understand him.

At the end of Norman Maclean's novella *A River Runs Through It*, Norman and his father are talking about the death of his brother, Paul. Paul, like Burley, had many characteristics of Jesus's prodigal "younger brother" and was killed in a bar brawl, but the details remained hidden. Norman and his father are trying to make sense of it all. Maclean writes,

> For some time, though, he [Norman's father] struggled for more to hold on to. "Are you sure you have told me everything about his death?" he asked. I said, "Everything." "It's not much is it?" "No," I replied, "but you can love completely without complete understanding." "That I have known and preached," my father said.
> Once my father came back with another question. "Do you think I could have helped him?" he asked. Even if I might have thought longer, I would have made the same answer. "Do you think I could have helped him?" I answered. We stood waiting in deference to each other. How can a question be answered that asks a lifetime of questions?[5]

In Port William, the Coulters could have had the same conversation about their family. There was both misunderstanding and love. I have learned that the same is true in congregational life. Even when a community agrees on vision and purpose, clarity on what it means to truly help one another remains elusive.

As a pastor, I find myself repeatedly asking the question, How can we move toward one another? If we truly are to be a community that loves one another (John 13:34), is devoted to one another (Rom 12:10), honors one another (Rom 12:10), builds up one another (Rom 14:19), bears with one another (Col 3:13), teaches (Col 3:16), forgives (Eph 4:2), is kind and compassionate to (Eph 4:32), admonishes (Rom 15:14), accepts (Rom 15:17), comforts (1 Thess 4:18), and encourages (1 Thess 5:11) one another, then we need to know one another. Reading *Nathan Coulter* reminded me of how intentional we must be to cultivate such a community. It does not just happen. Coffee and donuts after worship are great, but they are not enough. Being a family-size church is no guarantee of intimacy. Sometimes small is just small.

---

5. Maclean, *River*, 103.

All Swirling and Weaving

I don't believe a pastor can be expected to know *every* member at this level. The New Testament does not distinguish between the clergy and laity in these one-another passages. This is the whole church being the church for the sake of the church. As David Powlison notes, "We are to become a community where substantial conversations dominate."[6] But the church needs examples. Substantial conversations do not seem to dominate any regular aspect of most people's lives. And public discourse, at our present moment, seems to discourage anything that smacks of substance.

The current congregation I serve has a traditional reception line in the back of the sanctuary after each Sunday service. I extend the benediction and walk to the back before people begin filing out. In previous congregations, I avoided this. It seemed awkward to stand there and shake each hand, waiting for a compliment on the sermon like I had just gone 3 for 4 with a couple of doubles. Or perhaps even more awkward: shaking hands and waiting for the compliments that never come. But the practice of looking people in the eye every week and shaking their hand (or hugging the huggers) has allowed me to consider how the good news just proclaimed comes to bear on the specifics of their lives. Bob and Joanne as they give up their home of over sixty-five years to move into assisted living. Harold and Betty as they watch their daughter suffering from cancer, knowing they will likely outlive her. Ann as she cares for her mother with dementia. Jesse as he finishes his final year of high school.

This past Sunday, John shook my hand with his huge right hand. He shakes hands with purpose. He looked at me with even more intensity than usual and said, "I have questions." I attempted to deflect and responded, "I don't know if I have any answers, but let's get together."

As people began heading home or to Perkins for lunch after coffee, John and I sat at a table in the corner. I asked him what was on his mind. He said he has never been great at understanding the Bible. He said he reads it, and he struggles to understand the language and the customs. But something happened today. He said, "The passage this morning made me question: What purpose do I have in my life? I do things each day and I'm not sure I have been living in any direction."

I asked if he had any sense of what specifically there was about today's passage that caught his attention? He said, "During the sermon I felt like God was telling me to do something, but I don't have any idea what." Then

---

6. Powlison, "Pastor as Counselor," 25.

The Membership

he told me he had attended a men's retreat in the mid-1990s. He said, "The speaker that day was able to reach right into your heart with his words and grab a hold of you." He continued, "That was a turning point in my life—I wanted to be a better husband and person and made a commitment to do so. Then the years go by, and I think things just have lost focus."

We talked a little longer and then we both had to move on with the day. I asked him if he would like to get together on Thursday for coffee to talk more. He said he would like that. I don't know where this will go. After fifteen minutes, I now know more about John than I learned from any previous interaction with him. I know he is attuned to the Spirit. I am encouraged by the reminder that God is still at work through his word. These moments are holy and a gift.

I long for more conversations like this.

Drawn from a Different Well

James McBride's *The Heaven and Earth Grocery Store*[1]

> And they sang a new song, saying:
> "You are worthy to take the scroll
> and to open its seals,
> because you were slain,
> and with your blood you purchased for God
> persons from every tribe and language and people and nation.
> You have made them to be a kingdom and priests to serve our God,
> and they will reign on the earth."
>
> REVELATION 5:9–10

EVEN THOUGH I WAS a Presbyterian, we had Baptists and Catholics and Charismatics and Methodists and nondenominationalists worshiping every Sunday. We gathered for Bible study and dinner every Wednesday night, served our community, and went ice fishing on Kersey Lake—together. Yellowstone Presbytery ordained me as the pastor of Mount Republic Chapel of Peace, an interdenominational congregation two miles from the northeast entrance to Yellowstone National Park.

The mix of our membership came about by necessity. Unlike in most communities there weren't other options. We were intentionally interdenominational because we were the only church in a radius of over sixty

---

1. This chapter began as a short reflection published in *The Presbyterian Outlook*, January 2024, under the title, "Taking a Stand on Unity." Excerpts from that article are reprinted here with permission.

miles. You had to drive an hour and half in any direction to find another congregation. Diversity had been written into the bylaws: We were there for everybody. This was a gift.

The quaint log cabin chapel and our parsonage were nestled at the base of ten-thousand-foot Mount Republic between Cooke City and Silvergate, Montana. The locals referred to our backyard as Moose Meadow because we had a visiting moose at least twice a week, year-round, walking in the wetlands a few dozen feet from our back deck.

Cooke City is a snowmobile destination. Gallatin National Forest to the east of town is perennially ranked among the top five places in North America to find chest-deep powder. There are groomed trails, but they serve only as access to the numerous bowls and mountain faces of the backcountry that thrill seekers come to ride in. Snowmobiling in three feet of fresh snow is akin to carving through water on a jet ski—you must keep the throttle down fast enough to float on top.

Cooke City is also ten miles from Lamar Valley in Yellowstone. The valley is where the first pack of wolves were reintroduced into the park in the mid-1990s. The Druid Peak pack of Lamar Valley became famous and people moved to Cooke City in order to follow the pack. Wolf watching became a lifestyle. People would wake up early every morning before work and travel into the valley with long telescopes and binoculars to keep track of the wolves. Park Rangers numbered each wolf. A few residents had the numbers of their favorite wolves on their license plates, like Chicago Cubs fanatics.

Both snowmobilers and wolf watchers were drawn to the remote, rugged landscape of the Beartooth Mountains and the treasures they contained. But they rarely had similar views on political issues. The joke was that snowmobilers drove pickups and wolf watchers drove Subaru Outbacks. We had both wolf watchers and snowmobilers at Mount Republic Chapel of Peace. Politically, we were a purple congregation.

Katie and I took full advantage of everything the community had to offer. In the summer we went fly fishing, hiking, backpacking, and wolf watching. In the winter we went snowmobiling and cross-country skiing and ice fishing. Our daughter, Addie, and our dog, Boswell, both rode on snowmobiles before they were two months old. We enjoyed the outdoors with members from the church. The Republican members were not afraid to tell us they were Republican and why. The same was true with the

Democrats. As always happens when you develop deep relationships, you find out people are more complex than labels. Everyone has a backstory.

My pastoral instinct told me you could love Jesus and vote for a Democrat, and you could love Jesus and vote for a Republican. Caring for the congregation at Mount Republic Chapel of Peace confirmed this. I also found that cancer and marriage conflicts and teenage angst and the ravages of addiction were no respecter of political or denominational affiliation. Jesus came to heal our sins and walk with us in our sufferings. Jesus is for everybody. So is his church. This seems straightforward. So why, I still wonder, does it prove to be so complicated? We arrived in Cooke City in 2005. I realize the stakes have changed in the past two decades. Heated policy differences have given way to far deeper divisions. *Politics* may no longer accurately define what we are experiencing in America. This is all the more reason for the gift that is the diversity of the church to be nurtured, modeled, and celebrated.

The Bible begins, "In the beginning, God created the heavens and the earth" (Gen 1:1). The phrase "heavens and earth" is a literary device—a merism, where two opposite parts are used to represent the whole. "Heaven and earth" is another way of saying "everything." God created everything, seen and unseen, as we say in the Nicene Creed. In the middle of the Bible, the prophet Isaiah describes a new heaven and a new earth (Isa 65:17, 66:22). At the end of the Bible, John the Revelator is given a vision of that new heaven and new earth (Rev 21:1). Creation. Fall. Redemption. New Creation. That's the storyline.

I picked up James McBride's latest novel, *The Heaven and Earth Grocery Store*, partly because of the title. It's a mystery story that takes place in the Chicken Hill community of Pottstown, Pennsylvania. The novel begins in 1972 when Pennsylvania State Troopers visit the home of an elderly Jewish man named Malachi the Dancer. The troopers had found a mezuzah at the bottom of a well near Malachi's home, along with a human skeleton. A mezuzah is a piece of parchment with verses from the Hebrew Bible that many Jewish families attach to their doors. The mezuzah found at the bottom of the well had an inscription on it in Hebrew, "Home of the Greatest Dancer in the World." The Troopers don't receive much help from Malachi. The next day Hurricane Agnes knocked out the entire community and flooded the well and the skeleton and demolished any evidence there might have been from a cold case dating back to 1925. The rest of the novel tells the story of how the skeleton and the mezuzah ended up in that well.

Drawn from a Different Well

Like other McBride novels, *The Heaven and Earth Grocery Store* is full of characters you won't soon forget. They have quirks and faults and good intentions that don't always lead to action. They remind you of people you know. At the center of the story is a man named Moshe, who owns the local theater, and his wife, Chona, who runs the Heaven and Earth Grocery Store. Moshe and Chona are Jewish and live in the Chicken Hill neighborhood. Most of the Jews had moved out of Chicken Hill as the Black population moved in.

Early in the novel, Moshe and Chona have several arguments about moving downtown. Moshe's theater has had a run of success ever since he opened it up to Black bands. He wants to upgrade.

> "How can you sell Heaven and Earth?" she laughed.
> Moshe did not see the humor. "You don't have to spend your life selling kosher cow meat and onions to coloreds. Let's close the store. The Jews are leaving the Hill. Let's follow them."
> "Where?"
> "Down the hill to town. Where the Americans are."
> "Which Americans?" . . .
> "But the Jews are leaving Chicken Hill." (Moshe)
> "Ten blocks from here is leaving?" (Chona)
> "You know what I mean. Let's go where they are. They're our people."
> "Moshe, I like it here. I grew up in this house. The postman knows where I live."
> Exasperated, Moshe pointed out the kitchen window toward Pottstown below. "Downhill is America!"
> But Chona was adamant. "America is here."
> . . . His hands were on the table cradling a cup of tea. She gently placed one of her hands over his. "Don't you see what they have, Moshe? Don't you see *the well they draw from?*"[2]

It is a question that lies at the heart of the story. Where is America? Is it downhill where the "pasty-faced Presbyterians" lived?[3] Or on Chicken Hill? Chona's question gets repeated by Doc Roberts when he returns to Pottstown after medical school to find his home had become "a town of immigrants. Greeks who drove trucks, Jews who owned buildings, Negroes who walked Main Street like they owned it, Russians, Mennonites,

---

2. McBride, *Heaven*, 22, 27; my italics.
3. McBride, *Heaven*, 26.

Hungarians, Italians, and Irish."[4] Doc asks, "Where was America in all this? Pottstown was for Americans. God had predestined it. The Constitution guaranteed it. The Bible had said it."[5] Doc becomes an easy character to hate. His racism and decades-long grudge against Chona for slighting him in high school would be a cliché, if it weren't so believable.

The narrator describes Doc Roberts as "a good Presbyterian." He, like Chona, suffers from childhood polio and walks with the same limp she does. His limp gives him away when he walks the streets with a white sheet and hood hiding his face with the rest of the Pottstown Knights of the Ku Klux Klan. The repeated question in *The Heaven and Earth Grocery Store*, Where is America? invited me to ask a similar question: Where is the church?

Chona's observation that the Black citizens of Chicken Hill have something more than the Presbyterians downtown is based on her recognition that they "draw from" a different well.[6] It is clearly a metaphor, but wells play a major role in the story. The good old boys downtown refuse to provide a well for the Chicken Hill neighborhood. The original builders of the local synagogue had to tap into the water supply of one of the farmers further out of town. The well for the new synagogue becomes the crime scene of the cold case the novel starts with. Chona sees wealth of a different kind in the African American community, even when the town wouldn't afford them running water.

Chicken Hill is comprised of Eastern European Jewish immigrants and Blacks who moved north in hopes of finding something better in Pennsylvania. McBride writes,

> instead . . . [they lived] in a tight cluster of homes enclosed by the filth of factories that belched bitter smoke into a gray sky and tight yards filled with goats and chickens in a part of town no one wanted, in homes with no running water or bathrooms. Living like they were down home. Except they weren't down home. They were *up* home. And it was the same.[7]

McBride describes the conditions of Chicken Hill in a sentence that takes up thirteen lines, almost half the page. The sentence contains eleven commas as the details of squalor come to a crescendo. Then, in four short sentences

4. McBride, *Heaven*, 122.
5. McBride, *Heaven*, 123.
6. McBride, *Heaven*, 27.
7. McBride, *Heaven*, 87.

he summarizes their plight. The Black citizens of Pottstown moved north full of hope. They only found more of the same. But their resolve remains. This is why Chona doesn't want to move.

The residents on Chicken Hill draw from more than just their ethnic diversity. In the acknowledgments, McBride confides that the book began as an "ode to Sy Friend, the retired director of The Variety Club Camp for Handicapped Children in Worcester, PA.[8]" McBride notes that he worked at the camp for four summers while he was in college. He says, "Sy's lessons of inclusivity, love and acceptance—delivered not with condescending kindness but with deeds that showed the recipients the path to true equality—remained with" him the rest of his life.[9] The influence of the camp is clear in the story as the central characters also navigate life with physical handicaps. Chona has childhood polio and walks with a limp. She also suffers from sporadic seizures. Dodo, the young boy who witnesses Doc Robert's attempted sexual attack on Chona, is deaf. Dodo's friend in the Pennhurst Asylum for the Insane and Feeble Minded, whom Dodo affectionately names Monkey Pants, has cerebral palsy.

McBride's novel is as much an indictment of the treatment of those with mental and physical disabilities as it is of racial and religious prejudice. Just the name of the asylum is a reminder of the inhumanity of past practices. The novel is more than an indictment; it is an invitation to reconsider why we think purity—racial, physical, political, theological, or otherwise—is the goal? Dodo's inability to hear and Monkey Pants's inability to speak or fully control his body does not stop them from creating a complex communication system that provides a haven from the cruelties they experience at the asylum.

The God who created heaven and earth seems committed to diversity. The eternal community of God's people is comprised of "persons from every tribe and language and people and nation" (Rev 5:9). Biodiversity is what makes a natural space healthy. Since preaching a series on the book of Isaiah several years ago, I have always wanted to write an essay exploring the various flora and fauna found in Isaiah's prophecies. Isaiah speaks of cucumber fields, oaks of Bashan, cedars of Lebanon, crocuses, ostriches and jackals, lions and dragons, leopards and even hedgehogs. The new heaven and the new earth will be a place where the wolf and the lamb lie together, and where kids play with poisonous snakes (Isa 11). The thorns and thistles

---

8. McBride, *Heaven*, 383.
9. McBride, *Heaven*, 383.

will give way to junipers and myrtle (Isa 55). Author and farmer Wendell Berry has been making the case for decades that the health of the farmer, the soil, the neighboring ecosystem, and the consumer are all dependent on the diversity of the crops and those who tend them. In my home state of Iowa, where I am surrounded by thirty million acres bearing two crops, feed corn and soybeans, I regularly hear reports of how our rivers are dead or dying even as seed and fertilizer companies promise more and more yield. Purity can kill.

My second call was to First Presbyterian Church of Aberdeen, Washington. Aberdeen was formerly a fishing and timber town. At its height, it was home to over thirty-seven sawmills. When we arrived in 2009, three remained. The community was economically (and in most other ways) depressed. A tent encampment occupied by homeless people was established two blocks from our church building. We hosted the local Crystal Meth Anonymous group twice a week. The community foodbank was housed in our building's basement. It was not uncommon for someone living on or close to the streets to walk in on a Sunday morning during worship, looking for a warm place to get out of the rain. Many of them suffered from mental health issues and addiction; it was often unclear which led to the other.

One Sunday, a woman came into the sanctuary at the start of my sermon and walked all the way to the front-row pew. Something most Presbyterians are unwilling to do. She talked with me through the first ten minutes of the sermon, asking questions I tried to address quickly in parenthetical asides. Then she got up to leave. She was done. I wasn't. I asked her if I could pray for her before she left. She asked for prayer for her eyesight. So, I paused the sermon and prayed for her eyes. After the prayer she took off her glasses and walked down the central aisle declaring that she had been healed. I have no verification of this medically, but I still chalk it up privately as my first healing. After her departure, I picked up the frayed threads of my sermon where I had left off.

While I became used to the interruptions, I initially only saw them as interruptions. I had a sermon prepared, a message to deliver. I had a job to do. Over time, however, I came to see the interruptions as invitations. Where was the church? Was it up the hill where I lived, safe from the perennial flooding of the flats? Or was the church in the streets? Could it be both?

In my twelve years of ministry, First Presbyterian Church became economically, educationally, theologically, and politically diverse. I remember reflecting with a mentor that if someone took a random sample of our members' Facebook posts nobody would believe that this group of people could belong to the same church. According to the cable news pundits, we should have hated and feared each other. Instead, we worshiped and served as elders and shared meals and replaced the siding on the west side of the building together.

I told my mentor I had the sense that everyone assumed I was on his or her team. I often wondered if I was speaking out of multiple sides of my mouth. After talking this through, he suggested that this was likely because through the ministry of First Presbyterian they were encountering Jesus. Jesus sometimes sounds "conservative" and sometimes sounds "progressive" and most of the time Jesus is something different altogether. He challenges every human system. He refuses to be absorbed into a political agenda. Part of my job, it seems, is to follow him right into the welter of ambiguities.

I remember Michael Frost and Alan Hirsch describing how a congregation that had found the heart of the gospel was like a well in the middle of a desert. Once people found the well and tasted the goodness of the water of life, they kept coming back no matter how much they differed from one another.[10] Where else would they go? "You have the words of eternal life," Peter said (John 6:68). Looking back, we did not have any intentional strategy. I held tight to the conviction that if anything could unite us amidst our differences it had to be Jesus. We were willing to see how far we could push that conviction. Grace is a scandal because grace is a gift. And the Giver is generous. Grace can reach anybody. This was our great hope. It still is.

This past Christmas Eve in Des Moines, we held our traditional candlelight service of Lessons and Carols. The choir sang. Family members from out of town filled the pews. We heard the story of Jesus's birth promised in Isaiah and then fulfilled in Matthew and Luke. We sang our favorite carols. The Scripture readings and the carols seemed to warm up the congregation and as I began to preach, I could sense that the Holy Spirit was already at work. People stopped shifting in their seats. Hands began to rest quietly in laps. The midwinter coughs and clearing of throats ceased. The words I had prepared came clearly and I found a good cadence, anticipating the next line as I finished each sentence. Then, about midway through my message, our neighbor John walked into the sanctuary. John is probably in his fifties and a big man, six feet four, with developmental challenges. He walked in

---

10. Frost and Hirsch, *Shaping*, 47.

All Swirling and Weaving

on this cold Christmas Eve night in his bathrobe; he wasn't wearing any shoes. He walked to the front of the sanctuary and sat down in the second row as he often does (the pew is always open). As I continued to speak, John barked out unintelligible grunts. The eyes of the congregation, and the visitors they brought, moved from me to him.

Mara is one of our veteran saints. She was sitting with her husband and their son and daughter-in-law three rows behind John. Mara can't weigh much more than a hundred pounds. Her husband and family come to the church building once a year. On Christmas Eve. As I tried to finish my message, Mara got up, left her family, and came and sat next to John. She took him by the hand. She quietly talked to him and showed him where we were in the service in her bulletin. I finished my message. Before we closed the service with "Silent Night" by candlelight we celebrated Communion.

I gave my typical invitation to the table by explaining that the table didn't belong to me or to Union Park Presbyterian Church. The table belongs to Jesus. And Jesus has already covered the cost. We passed out the white bread that is so dry it sticks to the roof of your mouth and Mara helped John take a piece from the tray. Then we passed out the little cups filled with cheap grape juice. John took his little cup and after looking at it for a second, he held it high in the air and shouted in the clearest voice I have ever heard from him, "Alright, shots!" I could see my kids in the back of the sanctuary having a hard time controlling their laughter. I did too. When everyone had been served, I held out my cup toward the congregation as if I was making a toast and I reminded them that this was indeed the cup of salvation. I invited them to drink. John stood up and thirstily drank down the blood of Christ.

A few days later was the final Sunday of December. During our service we spent time sharing where we had seen God at work in our church family over the course of the year. Several people shared. It was encouraging. Then Sandy stood up and said that Christmas Eve was the highlight of her year. She said it was the most moving Christmas Eve service she had ever attended. And it had nothing to do with my message or the carols and candles. It was only five days later, but even *I* couldn't remember what I said that night. Where is the church? I don't know, exactly. It is here and there and in places we least expect it. What will the new heaven and the new earth look like? I don't know that either. But I think those of us who came to the candlelight service at Union Park Presbyterian Church that night got a little taste of it. None of us is likely to forget the Christmas Eve we drank shots of grape juice with John, in his bathrobe and bare feet, in the name of Jesus.

Onesies and Twosies

Barbara Kingsolver's *The Bean Trees*

This is what we have to offer to the world, is it not? A love unrestrained by success or timetables or ambitions.
Andrew Barber, "Tolkien and the Long Defeat"

WE USED TO PLAY a game with dinner guests called Bookish Balderdash. We would gather random books from around the house—kids' books and novels mostly. Each person would take a turn leading a round of play. The leader would select a book from the pile and write down the first sentence of the book. Everyone else would make up their own first sentence based on the brief synopsis on the back cover. The leader would mix up all the slips of paper and read all the sentences. Each person would then guess which sentence they thought was the true opening to the novel. You would get a point for every person who selected your made-up sentence and if you guessed the actual sentence, you would receive two points. We really know how to party! The beauty of the game was that many of the actual opening lines were as outlandish as the group's made-up ones.

Celebrated opening lines abound. Some are famous like "Call me Ishmael"[1] or "It is a truth universally acknowledged, that a single man in possession of a good fortune, must be in want of a wife."[2]

---

1. Melville, *Moby-Dick*, 11.
2. Austen, *Pride and Prejudice*, 49.

Some are humorous: "There once was a boy called Eustace Clarence Scrubb, and he almost deserved it."[3]

Some are bare statements of fact to orient the reader: "The Salinas Valley is in Northern California."[4]

Others reveal the personality of the narrator: "If you really want to hear about it, the first thing you'll probably want to know is where I was born, and what my lousy childhood was like, and how my parents were occupied and all before they had me, and all that David Copperfield kind of crap, but I don't feel like going into it, if you want to know the truth."[5]

Some summarize the entire novel: "History has failed us, but no matter."[6]

And some are unassuming but go on to introduce what become cultural icons: "Mr. and Mrs. Dursley, of number four Privet Drive, were proud to say that they were perfectly normal, thank you very much."[7]

Barbara Kingsolver's first novel, *The Bean Trees*, introduces us to Taylor Greer with this: "I have been afraid of putting air in a tire ever since I saw a tractor tire blow up and throw Newt Hardbine's father over the top of the Standard Oil sign."[8] By the time I finished page one, I was convinced I could listen to Taylor tell any story about any topic. Poor Mr. Hardbine survives but loses his hearing. You know that Taylor is young because she refers to him as "Newt Hardbine's father" and not by his name, the same way all the kids in our neighborhood call me "Isaac's dad."

Mr. Hardbine's flight to the Standard Oil sign is the catalyst for young Taylor (at this point in the story her name is Marietta) to begin thinking about her future:

> Newt Hardbine was not my friend, he was just one of the big boys who failed every grade at least once and so was practically going on twenty in the sixth grade, sitting in the back and flicking little wads of chewed paper into my hair. But the day I saw his daddy up there like some old overalls slung over a fence, I had this feeling about what Newt's whole life was going to amount to, and I felt

---

3. Lewis, *Dawn Treader*, 1.
4. Steinbeck, *East of Eden*, 3.
5. Salinger, *Catcher*, 1.
6. Lee, *Pachinko*, 3.
7. Rowling, *Harry Potter*, 1.
8. Kingsolver, *Bean Trees*, 1.

Onesies and Twosies

sorry for him. Before that exact moment I don't believe I had given much thought to the future.

My mama said the Hardbines had kids just about as fast as they could fall down the well and drown.[9]

Taylor's future goals are confined to avoiding getting pregnant like the other teenage girls in her small Kentucky town, and to never having to inflate a flat tire. She buys a car with no glass in the windows and heads west. Her plan is to change her name to whatever town she ends up in when the gas tank runs empty. Manifest destiny. She pushes past Homer, Decatur, and Blue Mound and coasts into Taylorville "on ... fumes."[10]

On her way west, Taylor stops for dinner at a wayside bar on a Cherokee Indian Reservation in Oklahoma. After eating her burger, she walks out to her car and finds a woman placing a three-year-old girl into the backseat of Taylor's car. The woman tells Taylor the child belonged to her dead sister and that no one knows, or cares, about her. Taylor retorts, "If I wanted a baby I would have stayed in Kentucky ... I could have had babies coming out of my ears by now."[11] The woman leaves and Taylor and Turtle (named for her penchant to grab hold of things and not let go) set out on their own.

The premise of the story is a little far-fetched. It is hard to care because one wants to believe that there might be someone out there with Taylor's hospitable approach to life. She leaves Kentucky to avoid becoming another statistic and forty-eight hours later she's a mother. Taylor takes it in stride even if she doesn't have any idea what she is doing. When she lands in Tucson, Arizona, she gets a job flipping burgers at Burger Derby. Her initial plan for childcare is to leave Turtle at the free Kid Central Station in the shopping mall and check on her every couple of hours during shift breaks.

Lou Ann Ruiz is also a Kentucky transplant living in Tucson. Her husband, Angel, left her a few months before Lou Ann was due to have their first child. Taylor comes across her ad in the newspaper for a roommate and the two new mothers join forces. When Taylor arrives in Tucson, her car breaks down and she finds herself rolling into a place called Jesus Is Lord Used Tires. The description of the tire shop gives you a sense of Kingsolver's playful tone throughout the story:

> Sprawled over the large corner lot was a place called Jesus Is Lord Used Tires. You couldn't make a mistake about the name—it was

---

9. Kingsolver, *Bean Trees*, 1.
10. Kingsolver, *Bean Trees*, 12.
11. Kingsolver, *Bean Trees*, 18.

painted in big, cramped blue letters over the door, with periods inserted between the words: JESUS.IS.LORD.USED.TIRES. On the side of the pleated tin building there was a large picture of Jesus with outstretched hands and yellow streamers of light emanating from His head. There was also a whitewall tire, perhaps added to the mural as an afterthought and probably meant to have no direct connection with the Lord, but it hung in the air below His left hand very much like a large yoyo. Jesus appeared to be on the verge of performing an Around the World or some other fancy trick.[12]

Jesus Is Lord Used Tires becomes the center of the action in the novel. Taylor's greatest fear is getting blown up by an overinflated tire and so, naturally, she ends up taking a job at a tire shop. Mattie, the proprietor, provides sanctuary for a refugee couple from Guatemala named Esperanza and Estevan. Their child, Ismene, was kidnapped by corrupt government forces and they fled to America in search of safety. Mattie's upstairs apartment is part of a southwest underground railroad of sorts for Central Americans seeking asylum. The shop also provides a community for a different kind of refugee in the likes of Taylor and Lou Ann from Kentucky. The result is an unexpected collection of friends—two single moms, Taylor and Lou Ann with Turtle and newborn, Dwayne Ray, along with Mattie, Estevan, and Esperanza.

I picked up *The Bean Trees* at the library on a whim. I was looking for *Demon Copperhead*, Kingsolver's latest novel, which was recommended by several friends. There was a twenty-three-week wait for the library's two copies of *Demon Copperhead* (I'm still waiting). I hadn't read *The Bean Trees*, and upon discovering that it was Kingsolver's first novel, I checked it out.

As a Presbyterian convinced of the often-veiled providence of God, I trust Austin Carty's notion that the right books tend to end up in our hands at the right time.[13] But I'm not sure I see any divine tea leaves revealing why *The Bean Trees* came to me when it did. It is a fun story. Fun is often in short supply. So, I read it.

The story is fun because Taylor is such a generous host as our narrator. We are introduced to the high desert of Tucson through her Kentucky eyes. Parenthood, political refugees, and friendship are all as new to Taylor as the reds and browns of the Arizona landscape. Through Taylor, Kingsolver is

---

12. Kingsolver, *Bean Trees*, 30.
13. Carty, *Pastor's Bookshelf*, 128.

Onesies and Twosies

able to hold two realities together: the surprising beauty of life and the brutal hardship of it. The story explores single parenthood, refugees and immigration, child abuse, and Native American adoption. I laughed through the entire story; not because she was making light of the meanness of life, but because Taylor wouldn't allow it to overwhelm her. And Mattie was doing something about it with her sanctuary for South Americans. And Lou Ann found some friends with whom to muddle through.

Taylor comes to grips with how little control she has as a mother after a scare at the local park. She tells Lou Ann, "I've just spent about the last eight or nine months trying to convince her [Turtle] that no one else would hurt her again. Why should she believe me now?" Lou Ann replies,

> You can't promise a kid that. All you can promise is that you'll take care of them the best you can, Lord willing and the creeks don't rise, and you just hope for the best. And things work out, Taylor, they do. We all muddle through some way.[14]

I originally thought that my role as a pastor was to help people do more than simply muddle through. Doesn't Jesus promise an abundant life?

I served a congregation in Cooke City, Montana, straight out of seminary. We were two miles from the northeast entrance to Yellowstone. Scott worked for the National Forest Service and attended services several times a year because his parents had a cabin in town. Scott is brilliant. He was heading up a study of wolverines the years we were in Cooke City. His vocabulary was humbling. He used all the SAT flashcard words in normal everyday conversation. Scott went out of his way to encourage me whenever he came to town.

Shortly after moving to Washington, I went back to Montana for a wedding. Scott was at the wedding, too, and I remember talking with him at the reception about how things were going. I complained to him about some of the struggles we were having, and I must have been wallowing in self-pity because at some point in the conversation he stopped me and said something like, "It seems to me that you are discovering that as much as we try to deny it, most of life is just a slog." Most people are forced to learn this long before I was.

I found myself in the slog of pastoral ministry. In my second year in Aberdeen, multiple churches partnered together and put on a weekend event. Church volunteers provided haircuts, groceries, a clothing bank, and

---

14. Kingsolver, *Bean Trees*, 168.

connected people to a variety of resources, programs, and social services. I handed out groceries for a while and then was asked if I would help in the prayer tent. A woman in her forties, with frayed blue jeans and a gray hoodie, asked for prayer for her teenage daughter and baby grandson. She was afraid that the father would hurt the child. I prayed as sincerely as I could for people I didn't know in a situation I didn't understand.

We committed to follow-up with everyone we prayed for, and a few days later I called the young grandmother. She told me her grandson had been shaken to death the night before. I didn't know what to say. I offered to help with a service. I met with her daughter and a few of her friends to plan a memorial in a local park. I found some musicians to sing "Amazing Grace." I said what I could to a gathering of teenagers. I had the sense that the memorial service was just another event in their lives, like homecoming, or a fight in the halls after fourth-period English class.

A month later I got a phone call from one of our elders at the church. Her son Kevin had died of an overdose. They found him in their bathroom that morning. He was in his mid-twenties. He was gifted and gracious and was a deep thinker. He was a writer and a musician. He had hundreds of classmates who loved him. They all gathered in our sanctuary for his funeral. The place was packed with a whole generation of kids from a town beaten down by a depressed economy.

It rains for nine straight months in Aberdeen. The weekend we interviewed, we saw multiple homes that had blue tarps on their roofs. I assumed they were temporary fixes after a recent storm. When we moved to town three months later, the tarps were still there. They weren't temporary. The blue tarps came to symbolize the languid sadness that seemed to hover over our community. I saw it again in the eyes of those kids who gathered for Kevin's funeral. This was not their first funeral for a friend who had died from an overdose, and it wouldn't be the last. It was my first. I said what I could and tried to give them room to grieve. I felt completely impotent.

These two funerals, back-to-back, made it clear that real ministry in Aberdeen was going to require something more than a nice mission statement and adequate parking.

I was buoyed by a group of pastors I met with on a weekly basis. We didn't agree on most things. We had different views on women in ministry, baptism, the continuation of spiritual gifts, speaking in tongues, the leadership structure of a congregation, political leanings, and the best approach to youth ministry. But we were in it together. We were all serving churches in the same forgotten place. We had homeless people sleeping on our front porches, in our parking lots. We had dozens of people in the throes of addiction to meth and heroin in our building multiple times a week. I met with this group of pastors to read Scripture together and to pray. We partnered with some of them to provide a local food bank and with others in attempts to support the local foster care programs. But mostly, I met with them to laugh. We enjoyed one another's company. We became more than colleagues.

If you asked me how ministry was going on any given day during our twelve years in Aberdeen, I would have answered with something equivalent to Lou Ann's "We all muddle through someway." That is what ministry feels like, most of the time. But we muddle through with hope.

The doctor in *The Bean Trees* explained to Taylor that Turtle had suffered a condition "called failure to thrive."[15] This is an accurate diagnosis of much of our community in Aberdeen—a failure to thrive. Turtle's doctor added, "It was completely reversible."[16] This is what keeps us going. The belief that at any given moment God might intervene in someone's life in a way they had never anticipated or imagined possible. And we saw it happen. Occasionally. Often through fits and starts. Most of what we did seemed small and insignificant compared to the sheer tonnage of pain that was all around us. Ministry felt like retreat. Like losing.

About five years into our time in Aberdeen, I read an article by Andrew Barber called "Tolkien and the Long Defeat." This short article gave me a vocabulary for ministry I didn't know I was looking for. The phrase "The long defeat" is how Galadriel, the Lady of Light in *The Fellowship of the Ring*, described the elves' attempt to protect Middle-earth over the centuries from the ever-growing shadow. When Frodo and the Fellowship arrive in Lothlorien, Galadriel tells Frodo, "The Lord of the Galadhrim is accounted the wisest of the Elves of Middle-earth. . . . He has dwelt in the West since the days of dawn, and I have dwelt with him years uncounted . . . together through ages of the world *we have fought the long defeat*."[17] Barber doesn't see this phrase as mere defeatism. Instead, fighting the long defeat is continuing to muddle through even when all practical wisdom would suggest otherwise:

15. Kingsolver, *Bean Trees*, 123.
16. Kingsolver, *Bean Trees*, 123.
17. Tolkien, *Fellowship*, 348; my italics.

> Tolkien has made his stand against the utilitarian spirit of the age.... Characters consistently make potentially catastrophic decisions simply because they believe it is the right thing to do.
>
> If anything, we find that most of the characters in *Lord of the Rings* cast their whole hearts into their endeavors. What they love is on the line: their friends and family, their gardens, a mug of ale in the company of friends. They hope and long for these things to be protected and offer themselves as sacrifices to make it so.
>
> In other words, if fighting the long defeat does not lead us to risk our reputations to love the outcasts, to stay with the chronically ill in love, to support ministry to those with Alzheimer's disease, or to prepare week in and week out for a one-person Bible study, we have misunderstood it. This is what we have to offer to the world, is it not? A love unrestrained by success or timetables or ambitions.[18]

I sat at my desk reading this three-page article, with an expensive library of commentaries, church ministry books, and Bible dictionaries on the shelves behind me. I realized this is the framework for the pastoral life that I needed: a love unrestrained by success or timetables or ambitions. I needed a picture of pastoral ministry that made a stand "against the utilitarian spirit of the age." I couldn't find that in the ministry books or church growth books that abounded. But 480,000 words of the long defeat in Tolkien's Ring trilogy was a start.

For several years our church committed to walk alongside those in our community who were addicted to methamphetamines and heroin. We opened our building up for a twelve-step group to gather twice a week. Slowly we began to open up our hearts to them as well. We made a meal for the group every Friday night. We partnered with a local social worker to offer parenting classes, anger management classes, and sober support classes for parents who had their children removed from their home. Eventually, we added some Bible classes and offered counseling. We worked with the local housing agency to try to find safe housing options. We provided childcare when people started regaining custody so they could continue to go to the meetings.

Central to all of this was a couple, Chris and Steph. We hired Chris on a part-time stipend from some grant money we received from our

---

18. Barber, "Long Defeat," para. 11–13.

denomination. His job description was basically to walk the streets of Aberdeen and encourage those who were in recovery.

Chris and Steph had their kids removed by the state a few weeks before they first showed up in my office. They were heading to rehab the next day and needed a place to sleep for the night. I had some extra "pastor's discretionary" funds that month and purchased a hotel room for them. They promised they would come back when they were finished with their thirty-day program in Tacoma. I had heard similar promises before and didn't expect to ever see them again. Thirty days later though, they were back in my office asking about starting a CMA (Crystal Meth Anonymous) group and using one of the church's rooms. Over time, Chris and Steph found an apartment and they found employment. They walked everywhere for two years because their licenses had been suspended. Two years, on foot, in the rainiest location in America. But they got their daughters, Christy and Zoey, back. Then they committed their lives to helping others do the same.

Jason, one of the church members on the oversight team, kept reminding me when I would get impatient with our progress, "Onesies and twosies. That is all we can expect. We're not going to solve the meth epidemic in our community overnight. Just one person at a time. Maybe two. Onesies and twosies." Ministry unrestrained by success or timetables or ambition.

The conclusion to *The Bean Trees* felt a little too tidy. The future for Taylor and Turtle and Esperanza, albeit fictional, is, of course, full of all the potential peril life has to offer the "foreigner[s], the fatherless or the widow[s]" (Deut 27:19) of the world. But Kingsolver leaves them all muddling through just fine at the end of her first novel. I recently got a notice from the library that *Demon Copperhead* was finally available. I finished it last week. Kingsolver's outlook has grown darker in the three decades since *The Bean Trees* was published. It is interesting that Taylor leaves Appalachia and moves westward in Kingsolver's first novel, and Demon is firmly planted back in Appalachia in her latest. The conditions Taylor was escaping have only deteriorated. The long defeat continues. This is why we need a happy ending on occasion. And laughter.

I caught up with Jason on our visit back to Aberdeen this summer. He has become the unofficial leader of the youth group. Mainly because his daughter Jenny is in high school and he wants her to have a youth group. There are only two to three high school kids in the church family but several more come to the gatherings. He told me Jenny had been collecting a small band of "misfit" kids at the high school and inviting them to their activities. Jason said one of the moms was talking to his wife, Amy, and told Amy that her daughter was a junior and never had a friend at school until Jenny sat by her one day during lunch. Jenny started a Dungeons and Dragons club at the high school and coordinates LARPing (Live Action Role Playing) games in the city park. These are the kids my friends and I would likely have relentlessly made fun of when I was in high school. To my shame, Jenny is inviting them into her life and then into God's kingdom. Onesies and twosies.

One Foot in Front of the Other

Alice McDermott's *The Ninth Hour*

I thank you, Father, Lord of heaven and earth, because you have hidden these things from the wise and the intelligent and have revealed them to infants.

Matthew 11:25

ALICE MCDERMOTT's *The Ninth Hour* opens with a recently fired Brooklyn Rapid Transit employee named Jim siphoning gas from the kitchen stove into his bedroom with a rubber hose and inhaling the gas until he asphyxiates himself. It is a jarring opening. The final sound he hears is something dropping to the floor in the apartment above him: "A sewing basket, perhaps—there was a thud and then a scratchy chorus of wooden spools spinning. Or maybe it was coins, spilled from a fallen purse."[1] We are never given the answer.

McDermott describes Jim's suicide as she does everything else in the novel. She writes with a detachment that allows uninhibited detail about any number of bodily functions but still evokes warmth and compassion. Detached warmth seems like a contradiction, but McDermott is an expert at dignifying the whole human condition. Her adjectives are simple, direct, often only one syllable and repeated throughout the novel. Dark. Dank. Pale. Damp. Thick. Soft. Sour. And yet she is unsparing in description, prodigious even.

---

1. McDermott, *Ninth Hour*, 7.

All Swirling and Weaving

Jim had pushed the couch in front of the door to prevent his pregnant wife, Annie, who was out shopping, from entering the apartment. He stands on the seat to check that the "transom above the door was tightly closed. Then he stepped down. He straightened the lace on the back of the couch and brushed away the shallow impression his foot had made on the horsehair cushion."[2] Why worry about crimped lace or an indention in a cushion moments before you take your own life? As Jim unhooks the gas line behind the stove, he worries about setting off the mouse trap they kept baited on the floor.

Annie left the apartment at four o'clock. By six, Jim is dead, and the leaking gas causes an explosion. Sister St. Savior, of the Little Nursing Sisters of the Sick Poor, has finished her shift begging for alms outside Woolworths and, uninvited, makes her way up the stairs as the firemen are writing their report. She finds Annie sitting on a bed in a neighbor's apartment. After a long embrace, Sister St. Savior says, "What we must do, is to put one foot in front of the other."[3] It is a helpful line and one any pastor would do well to employ in the right setting. Putting one foot in front of the other is often the most difficult thing for anyone to do. Sister St. Savior enters Annie's tragedy with a lifetime of experience and welcomed authority. Annie's first thought is where Jim will be buried. They are Catholic. He committed suicide. Even though they purchased a plot in Calvary Cemetery when they were married, she knows, "the Church will never allow it now."[4]

Sister St. Savior is set on getting him buried in Calvary. She tells Annie that they paid for the plot, they have the right to it. Over the years the nun had "collected any number of acquaintances who could surmount the many rules and regulations—Church rules and city rules and what Sister Miriam called the rules of polite society—that complicated the lives of women: Catholic women in particular and poor women in general."[5] But before they could get Jim buried *The New York Times* ran an article titled "SUICIDE ENDANGERS OTHERS." Jim would be buried in an unknown location in an unmarked grave because, Sister St. Savior said, "*The New York Times* has a big mouth."[6] Sister St. Savior handed off the nursing duties to a younger nun named Sister Jeanne. Sister Jeanne and Annie would

---

2. McDermott, *Ninth Hour*, 4.
3. McDermott, *Ninth Hour*, 13.
4. McDermott, *Ninth Hour*, 14.
5. McDermott, *Ninth Hour*, 15.
6. McDermott, *Ninth Hour*, 31.

become close friends. The Little Nursing Sisters of the Sick Poor would take Annie under their wing and give her work and companionship. Her daughter, Sally, would be raised, in part, by the nuns while her mother worked in the laundry.

Sister St. Savior's attempt to bury Jim through the church even though she knew it was against Catholic dogma of the time introduces a recurring tension in the novel. What claim do those on the front lines in ministry have over and against the institution? McDermott's narrator tells us, "She [Sister St. Savior] wanted him buried in Calvary because the power of the Church wanted him kept out and she, who had spent her life in the Church's service, wanted him in. Hold it out against the good I've done, she prayed. We'll sort it out when I see You."[7]

I used to go running with the manager of our town's soup kitchen. Mark and a host of volunteers served a hot lunch each day for those on or near the streets. Several years ago, they had to find a new location for their Sunday meal because the church that hosted the other days wanted their dining area and kitchen available for congregational fellowship after worship. We would run at night, after we put our kids to bed. My house was halfway up the hill and so we would always descend one of the steep roads into the downtown flatlands and take one of the side roads west toward the ocean. Aberdeen, at the time, had little nightlife and so the late-night runs provided a peaceful ending to hectic days. We ran at a pace that allowed conversation. Mark would often complain about the hierarchy of his denomination like members of *The Office* talk with disdain about "Corporate." When Mark was searching for a new kitchen location, I remember him saying, "It is such BS. They claim to be preaching the gospel, but we [the soup kitchen] are actually living out its values." His comment was akin to Sister St. Savior's remark to Annie on the way home from the non-Catholic cemetery where they buried Jim, "It would be a different Church if I were running it."[8]

The Ninth Hour provides a close look at the lives of one parish's nursing nuns in one borough of New York City in the early decades of the twentieth century. In that sense, it is as local as writing can be. Much of the action takes place in the convent laundry, in the basement. Annie is given a job helping Sister Illuminata washing clothes and rags where "there was, each day, the clear and certain restoration of order: fresh linens folded, stains

---

7. McDermott, *Ninth Hour*, 30.
8. McDermott, *Ninth Hour*, 63.

gone, tears mended."⁹ Each nun had a role. Some went out to the apartments to nurse. Others sat at storefronts collecting alms. Sister Illuminata put the laundry back to rights:

> Sister Illuminata was a wizard with a hot iron and starch, with scrub brush and bleach. On four dark shelves in a corner of her basement domain, she kept a laboratory's worth of vital ingredients: not merely the store-bought Borax and Ivory and bluing agents, but the potions she mixed herself: bran water to stiffen curtains and simples, alum water to make muslin curtains and nightwear resist fire, brewed coffee to darken the sisters' stockings and black tunics, Fels-Naptha water for general washing, Javelle water (washing soda, chloride of lime, boiling water) for restoring limp fabric. She had an encyclopedic understanding of how to treat stains. Tea: Borax and cold water. Ink: milk, salt, and lemon juice. Iodine: chloroform. Iron rust: hydrochloric acid. Mucus: ammonia and soap. Mucus tinged with blood (which she always greeted with the sign of the cross): salt and cold water ... She had four different irons of various sizes, which she washed on occasion in soap and water, then rubbed with sandstone and polished, lovingly, with beeswax.¹⁰

McDermott's catalog of laundering supplies is representative of her writing throughout the novel. Specificity matters. Sister Illuminata washes clothes to the glory of God. Presbyterians would proudly claim her; everything is decent and in order. It reminded me of Wendell Berry's critique of the farmers in Port William that discredit the profession by leaving their tools out overnight to rust in the elements or allowing the paint on their outbuildings to peel and flake. Like Berry's Kentucky farms, the convent laundry is sacred space. And though the "low-hanging light was dim, the dark brick walls clammy to the touch,"¹¹ the basement provides a window into the life and ministry of the convent.

The nuns minister to the sick and the poor of the city. The soiled sheets, menstrual rags, the coifs and veils of the sisters' habits represent the daily service. They are at once nurses, house cleaners, cooks, hospice caregivers, grief counselors, funeral planners, panhandlers, social and romantic matchmakers, and friends.

---

9. McDermott, *Ninth Hour*, 40.
10. McDermott, *Ninth Hour*, 41.
11. McDermott, *Ninth Hour*, 40.

One Foot in Front of the Other

The only reference to what happens upstairs in the sanctuary is the hours of prayer. The sisters stop what they are doing multiple times a day and gather to pray. But the novel takes place in the parish tenements and the basement laundry. In this sense, McDermott provides a glimpse behind the scenes. She gives unedited details of what it looks and smells and sounds like to care for people who can't care for themselves.

Ministry is rarely glamorous.

Sally spends most of her youth in the convent. While Annie works in the laundry or when the sisters let her go out to "catch her breath" in the afternoons, Sally spends her time with Sister Jeanne or Sister Lucy or playing with toys made of soap with Sister Illuminata. Sally assumes her calling is to one day join religious life. Becoming a novitiate means traveling to Chicago for training. The cross-country train ride provides Sally with all the introduction to humanity's squalor she can handle:

> Everything reeked. Of smoke and sweat and the human gas seeping from these mounds of flesh. . . . Unsteadily, she walked past her seat, to the end of the car—"pee cans," the dirty woman had said, vulgar—and then she turned around and walked back again. Here in the dim and smoky light were, for her consideration, a sampling of "the others" she was giving her life to: vulgar, unkempt, ungrateful. Pale, sleeping faces with gaping, distorted mouths, sprawled limbs, a hollow-eyed soldier looking out into the night . . . a yellow-skinned old man folded into himself, gazing forward with a murderous look. A young woman in a jaunty hat, chewing gum ferociously, reading a magazine, picking her nose and then flicking her fingertips into the aisle.[12]

As a girl Sally was transfixed by her reflection in the mirror wearing a black-and-white habit while playing dress-up in the laundry. The passengers on the train give her a glimpse into reality. She finds the prospect of caring for the sick and the lonely less appealing. New pastors are prone to similar presumptions.

The promise of preaching inspiring sermons to comfort the afflicted and afflict the comfortable was the initial impetus that led me to consider ministry as a calling. I believe my motives were pure. I wanted to introduce people to the sweeping vision of life presented in Scripture in much the same way that my favorite pastors and teachers had done for me. The earth is the Lord's and the fullness thereof. Through college and into seminary I

---

12. McDermott, *Ninth Hour*, 155.

All Swirling and Weaving

began to realize that one could spend a lifetime plumbing the depths of the gospel of Jesus. A whole creation is there to be explored and enjoyed. The fall, with its endless permutations of pain and sorrow, to navigate. Redemption to announce, with its glorious surprise of free grace. And the hope of a new creation that spurs us onward, albeit often only at the speed of one foot in front of the other. The story we are a part of is as wonderful and expansive as the living God who is writing it. I couldn't wait to begin.

Then Ron came to every Bible study and every committee meeting and every congregational gathering and raised his hand to ask the same two questions no matter how off topic they were for twelve straight years. And Joyce would make grown women in their sixties cry because they didn't clean the refrigerator in the church kitchen the correct way. And Marcy would pick up the Sunday school rooms every Tuesday morning and regularly remark that it would be a whole lot easier to keep those rooms straightened if we didn't have any kids around. I was never sure if she was joking or not. And Robert cheated on his wife. And James drank too much. And our youth pastor moved in with his girlfriend. And Kevin died of an overdose. And Linda was diagnosed with Alzheimer's. And on, and on.

This is embarrassing to say out loud, but for a long time I considered my congregation as an obstacle in the way of the ministry I was supposed to be doing. How could this group of people ever be considered an outpost of the kingdom of God here on earth? In C. S. Lewis's *The Screwtape Letters*, the demon Screwtape gives his nephew Wormwood the following advice on how to prevent his "patient" from becoming a follower of Christ:

> One of our great allies at present is the Church itself. Do not misunderstand me. I do not mean the Church as we see her spread out through all time and space and rooted in eternity, terrible as an army with banners.... All your patient sees is the half-finished, sham Gothic erection on the new building estate. When he goes inside, he sees the local grocer with rather an oily expression on his face bustling up to offer him one shiny little book containing a liturgy which neither of them understands . . . when he gets to his pew and looks round him he sees just that selection of his neighbours whom he has hitherto avoided. *You want to lean pretty heavily on those neighbors.* Make his mind flit to and from between an expression like "the body of Christ" and the actual faces in the next pew. . . . Provided that any of those neighbours sing out of tune, or have boots that squeak, or double chins, or odd clothes, the

patient will quite easily believe that their religion must therefore be somehow ridiculous.[13]

I confess this is how I saw my congregation. Not as "terrible as an army with banners." But singing out of tune with double chins and odd clothes. Thankfully, God is patient. Even with pastors.

Ministry took on a whole new sense of meaning when I recognized that the congregation was not an obstacle *to* ministry but, in fact, *was* the ministry I was called to. And I was one of them. A turning point in any parish ministry begins when the pastor stops referring to the congregation as *them* or *they* and instead uses *we* and *us*. We had plenty to do outside of the congregation for the sake of the community to be sure. God graced us with new people when we needed them, although never as many as my ego wanted. But the bulk of my calling was learning to follow Jesus together with this particular group of people, with all of our foibles, failures, and chins.

The Ninth Hour is a reminder that the church is a hospital. Early in his ministry, Jesus has dinner at Levi the tax collector's house. Mark tells us that "many tax collectors and sinners were eating with him and his disciples, for there were many who followed him" (Mark 2:15). The scribes and the Pharisees confront his disciples about this. Jesus responds, "It is not the healthy who need a doctor, but the sick" (Mark 2:17). Jesus is a doctor. Jesus is necessary because we cannot heal ourselves. This is why the New Testament metaphors of our new life in Christ are so dramatic. We were lost but now we have been found. We were blind but now we see. We have been born again. We were dead but are now alive.

On Friday nights our congregation in Washington would make dinner for the local CMA group that met in our dining room. When the meal was over, we would clean up the kitchen while the group started their meeting. The opening of the meeting was the same every week, like any twelve-step group around the world. "We admitted that we were powerless against crystal meth and our lives had become unmanageable." Our lives had become unmanageable. This was true for those of us who gathered on Sunday mornings as well. We would begin each service with God calling us to worship from a psalm followed by a hymn or song of praise. Then, week after week, we would confess that our lives had become unmanageable. We used more flowery language than the CMA group:

---

13. Lewis, *Screwtape*, 15–16; my italics.

All Swirling and Weaving

> Most merciful God,
> we confess that we have sinned against you
> in thought, word, and deed,
> by what we have done,
> and by what we have left undone.
> We have not loved you with our whole heart;
> we have not loved our neighbors as ourselves.[14]

I appreciate the cadence of the Book of Common Prayer but prefer the bluntness of the twelve-step liturgy. It is the same admission—though I am not sure if those of us who gather on Sunday mornings always recognize this. Another confession that we use includes the phrase "And apart from God's grace, there is *no health* in us."[15] Apart from God's grace our lives are truly unmanageable. This is an unexpected gift we have to offer the world—a safe place to acknowledge that we are *all* unwell.

A member of our church in Des Moines, Jolene, had a stroke a few days after Christmas this past year. The bleed was so massive it was inoperable. The critical care team didn't know how long she had, but there was nothing they could do to keep her alive. To free up rooms in the hospital, they moved Jolene to a hospice house a few miles from her home. I had never been there before.

The rooms were spacious and well furnished, allowing family members to stay twenty-four hours a day if they wished. Jolene's daughters sat at her side from morning till midnight every day for ten straight days. It was a long vigil. The staff was gracious and attentive. They knew that everyone who came to stay with them would never get well. People went to the hospice house to die. It was health care of a different kind. In a culture that hides death at all costs there was something refreshing about the lack of pretense. Outwardly we are all wasting away (2 Corinthians 4:16).

The words *hospice, hospital, hospitality,* and *host*el all share a clear etymological relationship. These are all places of rest and healing and welcome for the weary and heavy laden. The New Testament includes two passages that specifically list the characteristics required for elders in the church: 1 Timothy 3 and Titus 1. I don't think these lists are exhaustive, but it is noteworthy that they only list one gift that we would consider to be a leadership skill: the ability to teach. Everything else on the list is about character. Included in both lists is the word *hospitable*. The leaders in the church are

---

14. Episcopal Church, *Book of Common Prayer*, 320.
15. Anglican Church, "Morning Prayer," in *Book of Common Prayer*, 12; my italics.

One Foot in Front of the Other

expected to be hospitable, to be hosts, because the church is intended to be a hospital.

Sister Illuminata rinses and churns and beats the laundry all day, every day because she believes that a sister's calling is not "to credit her own soul with her sacrifice—her giving up of the world—but to become the sweet, clean antidote to suffering, to pain. 'You wouldn't put a dirty cloth to an open wound, would you?' Sister Illuminata said."[16] This perhaps sniffs a bit too much of an *us* and *them* distinction. As a Presbyterian, I find the more pessimistic sentiment, that even our most righteous works are filthy rags, more palatable. My experience seems more akin to the blind leading the blind than to being a "sweet, clean antidote," but there has always been an unexpected sweetness when I have had eyes to see it.

My father lives with us. He is in the middle stages of Alzheimer's and attends a day center twice a week that specializes in memory care to provide relief for at-home caregivers. I lead a short devotional at the day center twice a month when I drop him off. Some of the guests remember who I am and that I belong to Jay. Others ask me who I am and why I'm there multiple times during each twenty-minute devotional. Some raise their hand, or blurt out like eager second graders, to answer every question. Others never do. Don always sits in the front row. He never says anything, which is fine. Participation is not required. I can never tell if Don is engaging with the conversation or annoyed at my presence.

A few weeks before Christmas, I had the thought of closing our prayer time with the Lord's Prayer. I take prayer requests each week. Sarah asked me to pray for love. John, in his blue and gold Veteran cap, asked me to pray for safety for our troops. And for peace. Judy said she was thankful for the workers at the day center. So, I prayed for love and peace and safety and gave thanks for the staff and then invited everyone to join me in the Lord's Prayer. Everyone did. All twenty-five of them. Including Don. I live in Iowa, the Bible Belt's northern cousin, but I was still taken aback. We made it through the inevitable awkward mumbling that occurs in a mixed denominational setting, not knowing what version of the phrase "forgive us our debts/trespasses/sins" to use. And then we closed with "for Thine is the kingdom and the power and the glory, forever and ever. Amen." At "amen," Don rubbed his legs and then clapped his hands and stood up and shouted, "I like that. I feel good. Thank you." And then he sat down. This

---

16. McDermott, *Ninth Hour*, 90.

All Swirling and Weaving

was the best, and most passionate, response to the Lord's Prayer I have ever experienced.

The closing line of McDermott's novel comes at the end of a conversation between Sister Jeanne and Sally's children, the narrators—two generations descended from Jim who took his life in the opening chapter. Sister Jeanne gives an ambiguous reflection on the story's climactic moment which I won't spoil. Then she closes the novel with a quote from Jesus: "God has hidden these things from the wise and prudent, see? He's revealed them only to the little ones."[17]

In his book *The Imperfect Pastor*, Zach Eswine asks a series of gentle but probing questions every pastor, and Christian, must ask as we follow Jesus. One question reads, "Are we willing to forgo what works in the world for what Jesus teaches us to trust?"[18] In other words, do we really believe that the quiet, ordinary tasks of caring for the people God puts in front of us—body and soul—is enough? Can we trust the small, slow ways of God? Eswine confesses that early on in his pastoral life he quickly learned that in order to become "successful," he "needed to do something great, and [he] needed to define something great in terms of how large, famous, and fast" he could accomplish it.[19] Over time, Jesus taught him how to unlearn that definition and trust that "almost anything in life that truly matters will require you to do small, mostly overlooked things, over a long period of time."[20]

The title of McDermott's novel, *The Ninth Hour*, refers to the daily afternoon prayer at three o'clock. The Little Nursing Sisters of the Sick Poor would stop their work and gather in the sanctuary and pray. The thought of stopping what we are doing multiple times a day to pray is laughable in the world in which we live. There is too much to be done. The kingdoms of this world come with bombs and bulldozers. Jesus invites us to trust that mustard seeds and a pinch of yeast pack a bigger punch.

McDermott's care in detailing the grit and grime of the daily ministry of the Little Nursing Sisters of the Sick Poor challenged me to trust what Jesus teaches us to trust. God has hidden these things from the wise.

---

17. McDermott, *Ninth Hour*, 247. This is a quote from Matt 11:25.
18. Eswine, *Imperfect Pastor*, 61.
19. Eswine, *Imperfect Pastor*, 21.
20. Eswine, *Imperfect Pastor*, 26.

One Foot in Front of the Other

The Ninth Hour is a Catholic book. Catholicism, like Presbyterianism, has plenty of faults. But it has perhaps done a better job at defining and dignifying vocation than we Protestants have. The incontinence that comes with my father's dementia means our home laundry resembles Sister Illuminata's basement on a seemingly daily basis. I've yet to tackle his bed sheets with anything that would resemble her vigor and purpose. I am still learning how to put one foot in front of the other.

The ninth hour is also the hour of Jesus's death.

Circles and Circles of Sorrow

Toni Morrison's *Sula*

The past is never dead. It's not even past.
William Faulkner, Requiem for a Nun

When Nel Wright walks to Beechnut Park in the closing pages of Toni Morrison's novel *Sula*, she finds herself "not watching where she placed her feet" but heading to the "colored part of the cemetery."[1] She locates her childhood friend Sula's headstone. Sula is buried next to her mother, Hannah, her uncle, Plum, and her aunt, Pearl. Each headstone contains only their last name, Peace. "Peace 1895–1921, Peace 1890–1923, Peace 1910–1940, Peace 1892–1959."[2] The narrator makes this observation: "Together they read like a chant . . . they were not dead people. They were words. Not even words. Wishes, longings."[3] As the dates on the gravestones reveal, only one lived past their thirties. Peace did not come easy "up there in the Bottom"[4] of the fictional town of Medallion, Ohio.

The neighborhood known as the Bottom, even though it was up in the foothills, above the valley, was eventually razed to make room for the Medallion City Golf Course. The "nightshade and blackberry patches were [torn] from their roots"[5] like the history of the community that lived there. The novel acts, in part, as a kind of land acknowledgment. There was a

1. Morrison, *Sula*, 170.
2. Morrison, *Sula*, 171.
3. Morrison, *Sula*, 171.
4. Morrison, *Sula*, 6.
5. Morrison, *Sula*, 6.

neighborhood here before the Time and a Half Pool Hall was torn down. And Irene's Palace of Cosmetology. And "Reba's Grill, where the owner cooked in her hat because she couldn't remember the ingredients without it."[6] Morrison tells the story of the Bottom through the stories of two friends—Nel Wright and Sula Peace.

Sula is a different kind of book from the others in this collection. For those of us who grew up on stories about race like Disney's movie *Remember the Titans*, Morrison's writing can come as a shock. Sentimental inspiration is not her goal. I have lived and worked and worshiped in almost exclusively White spaces most of my life. There is much in *Sula* that is inaccessible to me as a reader without some help. Morrison invites me into the world of Nel and Sula, but the invitation is on her terms. She is not obliged to be concerned with my comfort level. My guess is challenging and stretching my comfort level was part of her motivation for writing. This chapter, therefore, will include more reflection on my process as a reader than the others. Reading this book has reminded me why reading in community, in intentional conversation with others, is so important. Especially in an historical moment when books by Morrison and others are being removed from libraries. Reading across cultural boundaries is one way the church can continue to learn to love our neighbors.

Nel was the daughter of Helene Wright, a woman who was respected, even feared, in the Bottom. She raised Nel in a strict, ordered home. "Any enthusiasms that little Nel showed were calmed by the mother until she drove her daughter's imagination underground."[7] Nel's father was a cook on a ship on the Great Lakes. He was absent her whole life.

Sula grew up in the chaos of the Peace household, under the loose authority of her mother, Hannah, and her grandmother, Eva. Eva had been married to a man named BoyBoy. The marriage was short lived. "During the time they were together he was very much preoccupied with other women and not home much. He did whatever he could that he liked, and he liked womanizing best, drinking second, and abusing Eva third. When he left in November, Eva had $1.65, five eggs, three beets and no idea of what or how to feel."[8] Two days later she left her three young children off at "Mrs. Suggs, saying she would be back the next day. Eighteen months later

---

6. Morrison, *Sula*, 3.
7. Morrison, *Sula*, 18.
8. Morrison, *Sula*, 32.

All Swirling and Weaving

she swept down from a wagon with two crutches, a new black pocketbook and one leg."[9]

Eva governed the household from her wagon on the third floor. The inhabitants included three fostered boys from separate families; Eva changed all their names to dewey. Three boys, each named dewey. And though they looked nothing alike they soon blended together and became known simply as "the deweys." She named a milky white "quiet man who never spoke above a whisper," Tar Baby. He was barely noticeable, existed on cheap wine, and "spent most of his time in a heap on the floor or sitting in a chair staring at the wall."[10] Morrison uses irony in the naming of her characters; they are unwilling to conform to European norms. The Peace household is anything but peaceful. Eva's ex-husband is a man named Boy-Boy. The whitest character in the story is Tar Baby.

What happened to Eva's leg remains a mystery, although the Bottom has its rumors:

> Somebody said Eva stuck it under a train and made them pay off. Another said she sold it to a hospital for $10,000—at which Mr. Reed opened his eyes and asked, "[Colored] gal legs goin' for $10,000 a *piece*?" as though he could understand $10,000 a *pair*—but for *one*?
>
> Whatever the fate of her lost leg, the remaining one was magnificent.... The wagon was so low that children who spoke to her standing up were eye level with her, and adults, standing or sitting, had to look down at her. But they didn't know it. They all had the impression that they were looking up at her, up into the open distances of her eyes, up into the soft black of her nostrils and up at the crest of her chin.[11]

Morrison's descriptions are at once horrifying and humorous. Her sentences are so well put together one almost forgets the brutalities she describes. Mr. Reed's off-color question about the value of one leg followed by the narrator's commentary about his question is intentionally playful. Even though they are talking about someone choosing to lose a leg in order to care for her family. This emotional complexity is a principal feature of Morrison's approach to storytelling. I laughed at the description of Eva's

---

9. Morrison, *Sula*, 34.
10. Morrison, *Sula*, 39–40.
11. Morrison, *Sula*, 31.

magnificent remaining leg and then stopped short, wondering if laughter was appropriate. Am I allowed to laugh at this? Am I supposed to?

Nel and Sula's friendship began in their dreams. "They were solitary little girls whose loneliness was so profound it intoxicated them and sent them stumbling into Technicolored visions that always included a presence, a someone, who, quite like the dreamer, shared the delight of the dream."[12] We are introduced to their friendship through the gaze of the men of the Bottom. "Pig meat" was the phrase Ajax used as the two girls walked by on their way to Edna Finch's Mellow House for ice cream.

Shortly after they had become friends, Nel and Sula were harassed by a group of Irish boys on their way home from school. As the boys confronted them, Sula took out a knife. But instead of using it on the boys, she chopped off her own finger and stared them down, no tears, no screaming. She calmly looked at them and said, "If I can do that to myself, what you suppose I'll do to you?"[13] It is a difficult scene. But the violence is not gratuitous. There is more at work here than shock value. Sula is acting out of defiance. Instead of waiting for the Irish boys' attack, physically or sexually, she cuts herself as a means of self-protection, and to protect Nel. Like her grandmother's leg, self-mutilation was a means of sacrifice for the sake of survival. The precision of Morrison's dialogue and the beauty of her sentences, combined with the challenge of scenes like this one, forced me to wrestle with my own assumptions. I had to look again, even at my own description in the sentence above: "She cuts herself as a means of self-protection." What kind of system creates an environment where self-mutilation becomes a strategy for survival?

The event that linked the girls together for the rest of their lives was a tragic accident. Nel and Sula were enjoying the freedom of a summer walk along the river. A young boy named Chicken Little joined them, and the three children climbed a tree. The narration slows down so much that I assumed that the boy would fall from the tree. He didn't. Instead, once all three children reached the ground, Sula began to swing Chicken Little around and around. He slipped "from her hands and sailed out over the water. . . . The water darkened and closed quickly over the place where Chicken Little sank."[14] The memory of the "closed place in the water" becomes a recurring refrain throughout the novel.

12. Morrison, *Sula*, 52.
13. Morrison, *Sula*, 55.
14. Morrison, *Sula*, 61.

All Swirling and Weaving

The burden of the secret of Chicken Little's drowning first propels the girls together and then drives them apart. Nel embraces a life like her mother's. She marries and settles down in Medallion, never to leave. Sula ventures out. She tries college and city life. Nothing takes. A decade later, Sula returns, as the narrator describes, "accompanied by a plague of robins."[15] The first thing Sula does is put her grandmother, Eva, in an asylum. Then she sleeps with Nel's husband. Wrecking the marriage and their friendship. When Sula dies, the narrator notes, "The death of Sula Peace was the best news folks up in the Bottom had had since the promise of work at the tunnel."[16]

This is a remarkable sentence and a clear example of Morrison's economy of language. The death of Sula Peace being good news for the folks up in the Bottom is a morbid declaration itself. Death should not be good news. The narrator's description of Sula's death as "the best news ... since the promise of work at the tunnel" succeeds on multiple levels; it is threaded with ironies. The promise of work at the tunnel was a false promise. The White migrants were given all the jobs, not the Black residents from the Bottom.

In the same way, there was hope that Sula's death would bring a kind of relief to daily life in the community. In fact, it only exacerbated the problems. Sula's presence had had a reforming power to it. Mothers "who had defended their children from Sula's malevolence ... now had nothing to rub up against. The tension was gone and so was the reason for the effort they had made."[17] Daughters of elderly mothers who saw Sula's mistreatment of Eva had taken better care of their own aging mothers-in-law. Now that Sula was gone, they regressed back to a "steeping resentment of the burdens of old people. Wives uncoddled their husbands ... and even those Negroes who had moved down from Canada to Medallion ... returned to their original claims of superiority" over the Southern-born Blacks.[18] An entire community reverting back to its most base instincts because the town pariah has died is oddly playful. And it works. This only seems to deepen the tragedy.

Reading *Sula* provoked a lot of questions. A primary one for me was, How do we who are comfortable walk with those among us who have

---

15. Morrison, *Sula*, 89.
16. Morrison, *Sula*, 150.
17. Morrison, *Sula*, 153.
18. Morrison, *Sula*, 154.

experienced unbearable suffering? Each character in the story responds to circumstances, past and present, that are unimaginable, compounded by the imposed limitations placed on the main characters' race and gender. "They were neither white nor male, and . . . all freedom and triumph was forbidden to them, [so] they had set about creating something else to be."[19] What is there to say in the face of such realities as racism, systemic exclusion, internalized violence, generational poverty?

I don't presume to know. The fact that Sula and Nel had the resilience to "set about creating something else to be" is a marvel. My first impulse was to consider how to "fix" this. Morrison isn't offering a fix, but a witness. Perhaps that is not entirely accurate. Morrison's work, in *Sula* and elsewhere, is an act of resistance. She is unwilling to allow polite narratives with uplifting conclusions to be the only historical account of America's racial past. Morrison is offering a correction. Part of her resistance is telling stories that don't contain tidy resolutions.

Sula ends with the haunting description of Nel walking home alone from the cemetery weeping for her friend: "It was a fine cry—loud and long—but it had no bottom and it had no top, just circles and circles of sorrow."[20] If Barbara Kingsolver's *The Bean Trees* reminded me that in the midst of the long defeat sometimes we need a happy ending, *Sula* confronts me with the reminder that tidy resolutions often never arrive.

As a pastor, I believe the narrative arc of Scripture, and therefore the arc of history, is one that comes to its completion in redemption. It is also true that only the first and last two chapters of the Bible (Gen 1–2 and Rev 21–22) go well. What we find in between is often as gritty as scenes from Morrison's novel. For reasons beyond our understanding, God does not seem to be in a hurry to "fix this." As I put *Sula* down, I wondered what in my own very different experience offered a similar challenge and allowed any kind of legitimate comparison.

Our congregation in Washington regularly offered a six-week Bible study on Wednesday nights throughout the year. Six weeks was a good rhythm. It allowed focused study over a determined period and then we would take a month off before starting something new. The Bible study included a simple soup dinner so families would get a night off from making meals. One year we did a manuscript study of six scenes in the Gospel

19. Morrison, *Sula*, 52.
20. Morrison, *Sula*, 174.

All Swirling and Weaving

of John. We would print the passage, double-spaced, on a single sheet of paper for each participant and remove the chapter and verse references. Someone would start with a prayer and then we would read the passage out loud. Everyone then had ten minutes to mark up the passage on their own—they were instructed to circle repeated words or phrases, underline conjunctions, and notice what they noticed. Everyone wrote down every question that came to mind.

After ten minutes, we went around the table and shared the observations and questions we came up with. We attempted to answer the questions together, to the extent possible, based solely on the passage without outside commentary or study Bible notes. How was the scene put together? What does John emphasize? Is the story primarily about something Jesus does or is it calling its readers into action? The key was not moving ahead too quickly. The best insights always came in the second half of the hour. The goal was to summarize the entire passage in one sentence.

We spent an evening with John 11, Jesus raising Lazarus in Bethany. It is a familiar passage. The temptation is to jump forward to the climactic moment when Jesus calls Lazarus out of the tomb. But John takes his time, forty-three verses before he gets there. He emphasizes Jesus's love for this family, for Martha, Mary, and Lazarus. He gives details about the crowd. Bethany was only two miles from Jerusalem, many friends had come to mourn. Twice, John tells us that Jesus was "deeply moved" (vv. 33 and 38). The NRSV and ESV translations have a footnote for this verb: it also means indignant. Jesus rages at death. A friend he loved had died too soon. Lazarus's sisters and the whole community were grieving. Famously, he weeps with them. But he does more than weep. He becomes indignant. Death is an intruder, the sharpest reminder that the world is not the way it is supposed to be. Jesus is the author of life. Death makes him angry.

As we sat around the table reflecting on Jesus's anger at death, I took stock of who was in the room. Nate's dad had been a favorite math teacher in the local school. When Nate was a teenager, his dad had died of a massive heart attack while teaching class one afternoon. Matt's brother taught English in a school in Iraq and was shot and killed by a student the year before. Ron and Joan's son had been murdered on the streets of our town when he was in his twenties. Tony's brother died when he was 21, Tony was 18 at the time. Jeff and Sara's mothers had each died of cancer when they were in their early fifties. Literally everyone in the room that evening, except for Katie and me, had suffered a sudden, tragic loss of someone they loved, way too early. As a congregation, these were the stories we held for one another. We went around the table and named their family members. It seemed significant to acknowledge that this was the group of people that gathered that evening to sit under this passage of Scripture.

God didn't solve anything that night. Nobody was healed of sorrow, as if such a thing were possible or even desirable. But I do know that the Lord of the text met us at the table that evening. There was comfort in remembering that Jesus raged at death too. The suffering of those present was not the same as the suffering described in *Sula*. I don't mean to compare the two, as if anyone's experience of suffering could be compared to others. But any ministry must learn how to walk with those who have suffered the unimaginable.

Part of my job as a pastor is to learn to sit with the pain of my members. The temptation is to demand redemption or comfort as quickly as possible. Let's fix this. But life doesn't work like that. Yes, Lazarus was raised. But he would die again. Some pain and brokenness will not be mended or restored this side of the new creation, even as we continue to work toward its healing. There are injustices that only final judgment will set right, and then, only in ways we can't begin to understand or venture to guess.

In John 16, Jesus says to his disciples, "I have told you these things, so that in me you may have peace. In this world you will have trouble. But take heart! I have overcome the world" (John 16:33). We need both sides of this statement. The world *is* full of trouble. Reading *Sula* was a stark reminder of this. "Trouble" is a soft translation. The NRSV uses "persecution." The KJV used "tribulation." And yet, it is also true that Jesus has overcome the world. The pastoral challenge is figuring out when to hold up which side of Jesus's claim.

In a previous congregation, one of our core leaders had an adult son who committed a horrific crime. It was the kind of situation in a small town that made it almost impossible for the family to continue to live there. And in less than a year they did end up moving away. The day after the arrest, I walked to Joanne's house to talk with her. As I knocked on the door, part of me hoped that maybe she wouldn't be home. When she opened the door, I froze and said something like, "I am sorry you are going through this. We are here for you." I couldn't find any other words I thought would help. So, I gave her a hug, and I walked back home.

I had been instructed by countless mentors that when you enter an impossible situation, you should not go in guns blazing with all the answers.

Just be present. It is wise counsel. Most of the time. Trite aphorisms like "All things happen for a reason" or "Remember that God works all things together for good" in such moments are not helpful. They often cause more harm. But giving the impression that the current situation is beyond God suggests that despair is the only option. This, too, is pastoral neglect. In my efforts to avoid oversimplification, I failed Joanne that afternoon. She didn't need answers or a fix. But she did need to hear from her pastor that God was still there, and that he was still good, and, somehow, still enough.

Cornelius Plantinga's book *Not the Way It's Supposed to Be: A Breviary of Sin* takes a 360 degree look at the brokenness of the world. Plantinga offers an unblushing look at the wreckage of human sin, but then he writes a bracing epilogue, full of hope. I return to it regularly when in need of ballast:

> Evil rolls across the ages, but so does good. Good has its own momentum. Corruption never wholly succeeds. . . . Creation is stronger than sin and grace stronger still. Creation and grace are anvils that have worn out a lot of our hammers.
>
> To speak of sin by itself, to speak of it apart from the realities of creation and grace, is to forget the resolve of God. God wants shalom and will pay any price to get it back. Human sin is stubborn, but not as stubborn as the grace of God and not half so persistent, not half so ready to suffer to win its way. . . . To concentrate on our rebellion, defection and folly—to say to the world "I have some bad news and I have some bad news"—is to forget that the center of the Christian religion is not our sin but our Savior.
>
> But to speak of grace without sin is surely no better. . . . In short, for the Christian church . . . to ignore, euphemize, or otherwise mute the lethal reality of sin is to cut the nerve of the gospel. For the sober truth is that without full disclosure on sin, the gospel of grace becomes impertinent, unnecessary, and finally uninteresting.[21]

Here is a description of the two sides of Jesus's claim in John 16:33. The world is full of trouble. Evil rolls across the ages. But Plantinga's insistence on the resolve of God is also true. The church, to be faithful to Jesus, needs to speak of the stubborn realities of sin. We need to name those realities and not "ignore, euphemize, or otherwise mute" them. *Sula* offers us vocabulary and imagination for the naming and challenges us to look again at what we thought we already knew. Nothing but honesty does justice to the

---

21. Plantinga, *Not the Way*, 199.

horrors people have experienced in America's racial past and present. But, somehow, we also need to continue to speak of the stubborn grace of God.

I remember David Powlison making an offhand comment in a lecture about the way the Bible presents the doctrine of God's judgment. He remarked that one might assume, listening to certain churches or traditions, that the most common use of God's judgment in the Bible is as a threat: Be good, or else. Scripture does include warnings. But more common is the articulation of God's judgment not as a threat but as a promise, intended to bring comfort. If you are the oppressed, under the thumb of the arrogant, the powerful, and the wicked, it is good news to hear that God will one day set the world to rights. This is why the Negro spirituals so powerfully used the imagery of Israel's exodus out of Egypt. In the face of unspeakable horror, God as deliverer is often the only hope. And if God is going to deliver, he needs to judge the oppressors. Psalm 37 reminds us,

> Do not fret because of those who are evil
> or be envious of those who do wrong;
> for like the grass they will soon wither,
> like green plants they will soon die away....
> A little while, and the wicked will be no more;
> though you look for them, they will not be found.
> But the meek will inherit the land
> and enjoy peace and prosperity. (Ps 37:1–2, 10–11)

In this psalm, the promise of judgment offers comfort and hope. But not for the oppressor. My tendency in reading such a psalm is to assume the opening phrase, "Do not fret," is talking to me, personally. The evil and wicked are those out there. What happens when we find ourselves confronted by the prospect that we, either by cultural participation or the inertia of indifference, should identify ourselves with the oppressor and not the oppressed?

I was recently talking with a friend about the current crises battering our world. It is early 2025, and so those include wars in Ukraine, Israel and Palestine, and Sudan. Everyday children are killed. We were talking about how we might even begin to process this. What do we say in the face of such wreckage? The conversation felt insufficient. The usual options, inadequate. Sure, we can call our congressional representatives. We can support relief organizations. We can read and educate ourselves on the issues. It all seemed small. The answer we landed on was the promise of new creation. New creation is not a small answer. Still, it sounded trite. Those families certainly want new creation; they want their children back. But not someday. Today. Yet something needs to be said about the resolve of God. Despair can't be the only option. God wants shalom and will pay any price to get it back. He rages at death too. And he willingly entered into its long, dark shadow himself.

I have only read three of Morrison's novels. I can't say they have been easy to read, despite the wonder of her prose. But they bear witness to a racial past that is still being worked out in the present. They speak of the stubborn realities of sin—something the church cannot hide from. Or fix. We can and must name it for what it is. And learn to sit with the pain for as long as it takes.

They Did Indeed Move in a Mysterious Way

David James Duncan's *The Brothers K*

The departure of the church-going element had induced a more humanitarian atmosphere.
Dorothy Sayers, Clouds of Witness

I READ THREE NOVELS this past year featuring protagonists who are seminary dropouts. Jayber Crow[1] leaves seminary in Louisville and becomes a barber in Port William. Noe Crowe[2] (maybe it's the last name) drops out, spends a summer with his grandparents, and turns into a romantic and a fiddler after working for a rural Irish electric company. Virgil Wander[3] quits school and moves to a small town on Lake Superior to purchase a dilapidated movie theater because he was "fresh out of God but had adequate cash." The authors—Wendell Berry, Niall Williams, and Leif Enger—could have selected any number of prior academic pursuits for their characters. And while it is often perilous to guess at authorial intent, there seems to be a subtle statement that something about the clergy or institutional religion is wanting. Seminary, in these stories, is something to leave behind.

My summer novel this year was *The Brothers K* by David James Duncan. I had previously started reading it twice before. I enjoyed *The River Why?* and several of Duncan's essays and I am a big fan of baseball and

1. Berry, *Jayber Crow*.
2. Williams, *This is Happiness*.
3. Enger, *Virgil Wander*, 93.

fishing and so I am not sure why it took me three attempts to get into the story. Once in however, I was quickly reminded of the rousing fun of Duncan's playful prose. You can feel the energy and chaos of the Chance family of eight on every page and with each escalating escapade. Duncan, for his part, is not subtle at all. He takes the institutional church head on. This isn't a surprise for those familiar with Duncan's nonfiction. His essay collection *God Laughs and Plays* carries the subtitle *Churchless Sermons in Response to the Preachments of the Fundamentalist Right*. In many ways, *The Brothers K* is Duncan's exploration of how such "preachments" impact the Chance family.

Kincaid Chance, named for a town in Oklahoma where his father played in the minor leagues, narrates the story of his family. His mother, Laura, is a devout Seventh Day Adventist. His father is not. Hugh Chance works in a lumber mill after a hand injury shortens his baseball career and spends his Sabbaths watching the Yankees. Kincaid is the youngest of four brothers and has twin sisters. Eventually Laura's commitment to the First Adventist Church of Washougal leads to a fissure in the family. Duncan clearly aims to explore the destructive elements of sectarian Christianity.

The Washougal Church and Laura's slavish commitment to all its teachings despite the damage it does to the family would appear to be a caricature. The church leadership falls into every expected abuse—manipulation, legalism, control, spiritual bullying, lies and cover-up, hypocrisy, sexual misconduct, and petty vengeance. Unfortunately, it rings all too true. *The Brothers K* was published in 1992 but there is evidence to suggest that fissures in families and congregations have only intensified. Russell Moore, who is currently the editor-in-chief at *Christianity Today*, said recently, "A pastor asked me the other day, 'What percentage of churches would you say are grappling with these issues (residual conflict over partisan politics, COVID-19, race relations, etc.).' And I said, 'One hundred percent. All of them. . . . I don't know of a single church that's not affected by this."[4] It makes one pine for the good old days of the worship wars and fights over sanctuary carpet colors. The disclosure of multiple high-profile pastors' moral failings, #ChurchToo sexual abuse and cover-up, and the deconstruction and "exvangelical" movements have only added to the complicated challenges of church ministry in America after the first two decades of the twenty-first century.

---

4. Alberta, "Politics Poisoned the Church," para. 34.

They Did Indeed Move in a Mysterious Way

The church, like many other institutions, is an easy target for criticism. The proximity of the name "God" to the designation "God's People" brings to the church a higher expectation of moral standards than other groups—Hell's Angels or the Mob, for instance. The standards should be high. "Speak to all the congregation of the people of Israel and say to them: *You shall be holy*, for I the LORD your God am holy" (Lev 19:2; my italics). In fact, God intended the beauty and goodness of the moral code to make the nation of Israel the envy of their neighbors.[5] The expectations of the New Testament people of God are the same. Jesus's bracing Sermon on the Mount includes the injunction, "Be perfect, therefore, as your heavenly Father is perfect" (Matt 5:48). The church and its individual members have always fallen short of God's glory.

Critique is both deserved and necessary. The church is reformed and (should be) always reforming. Entire books of the Bible are written with this critique in mind—see Jonah or 1 Corinthians or almost all of Jesus's encounters with the Pharisees in the Gospel narratives. Regular practices of confession, repentance and forgiveness, denominational polity (including accountability and discipline), as well as robust theological debate all assume the need for regular critique. A church, at its best, knows its darkest proclivities, proactively guards against them, and welcomes correction. In other words, the posture of the church should begin with humility, caution, and self-deprecation. The First Washougal SDA Church fails to hold such a posture in Duncan's novel.

Duncan offers at least two different layers to his critique of the church. The first is the reality that individuals and, by extension, institutions sin. *The Brothers K* has its own specifics but they are similar to what we find in the news on a regular basis. Pastors run off with their administrative assistants. Sexual predators find their way onto the youth group staff and the church leadership, out of fear of public perception, do the unconscionable and keep it quiet. Unregulated financial practices entice and then enable financial corruption. Members gossip about other members while folding the monthly newsletter in the office. Families hold the mission of the congregation hostage because of the power they have accumulated over years of service and giving. Fear prevents others from confronting those in power. These and countless other permutations plague the witness of Christ's church and do real damage to real people with real names and real lives. Lord have mercy. I understand the outrage. This type of wreckage is

---

5. See Deut 4:6–8.

already found in families, businesses, politics, youth sports leagues, and school boards; why would anyone volunteer to join a church where they will just find more of the same?

The second layer of critique in *The Brothers K* is not simply moral failure but a grinding, suffocating, legalistic environment. They offer no joy of the Lord, only the squashing of joy. No obedience of faith, only obedience by force and fear. Duncan captures within his story the essence of Steinbeck's description of Samuel Hamilton's wife in *East of Eden*: "A tight hard little woman humorless as a chicken. She had a dour Presbyterian mind and a code of morals that pinned down and beat the brains out of nearly everything that was pleasant to do."[6] As a Presbyterian pastor I feel I am at liberty to pick on poor Mrs. Hamilton, as humorless as a chicken, and I do not know why Duncan chooses a Seventh Day Adventist church for his novel but you could obviously replace these denominations with any others or with all of the nondenominational varieties as well.

The question Duncan's novel kept inviting me into was, What story are churches like these telling? And how has that story become so pervasive? I am unaware of Duncan's biography except for what he offers in his essays, but you get the clear impression that he grew up in a church much like his fictional First SDA in *The Brothers K*. The popular author Philip Yancey has made a career out of wrestling on paper with the faith he found despite the narrow doctrine of the church setting in which he grew up.[7] Writing as a means of recovery from spiritual trauma is a common thread in American literature.

I recently had a conversation with a member from our church named Sally. Sally and I share a mutual friend named Molly. I have been out of touch with Molly for a few months and so I asked Sally if she had spoken to her lately. Her response went something like this: "No I haven't. I know, I'm terrible. I've been meaning to talk to her for weeks now and I just haven't gotten around to it. I meant to email the whole group [friends from a former congregation] and try to get lunch together or something, but I haven't. And I know Jan [another friend] is not doing well and I keep trying to get over to visit her but with work and family, I just keep putting it off." In less than thirty seconds, my simple question sent her on a spiral of failure and guilt. I apologized and told her I had no intention of putting

---

6. Steinbeck, *East of Eden*, 10.

7. See especially *Soul Survivor: How My Faith Survived the Church* and his memoir *Where the Light Fell*.

any expectations on her. She replied, "Oh, I know, guilt is just my default position."

In my experience as a pastor, guilt as a default position is everywhere. Churches that confessionally proclaim grace alone through faith alone in the finished work of Christ alone are filled with members who feel they do not measure up or have not done enough. Or they turn faith into a work and question whether they believe enough or trust enough or are sincere enough. One winter, I served as an interim pastor at a church in Chicago. At least once a month, one gentleman would pull me aside and ask, "How do we know when we've given enough? How do I know if I've done enough?" And while guilt does serve a purpose in the Christian life and can be a sign of a healthy and active Spirit-filled conscience, something is off when it becomes the pervasive experience of those who hear every week, "Friends, in Christ, we are forgiven."

Sinclair Ferguson has helped me understand that this pervasive sense of guilt is not simply a lack of understanding of the grace of the gospel but ultimately a misunderstanding of the character of God. He writes,

> The root of legalism is almost as old as Eden, which explains why it is a primary, if not the ultimate, pastoral problem. In seeking to bring freedom from legalism, we are engaged in undoing the ancient work of Satan. In Eden the Serpent persuaded Eve and Adam that God was possessed of a narrow and restrictive spirit bordering on the malign. After all, the Serpent whispered, "Isn't it true that he placed you in this garden full of delights and has now denied them all to you?"[8]

What is happening in Duncan's fictional Washougal First SDA and from the pulpits of real churches and therefore in the minds and hearts of churchgoers is a misrepresentation of the Bible's most central character. When God is seen, in Ferguson words, as a "narrow and restrictive" killjoy, the church follows in his footsteps.

Ferguson offers a simple case study as a litmus test of what we believe to be the overarching story of the Bible. He asks his readers to consider the claim, "God loves me because Christ died for me?"[9] At first glance it appears to have the elements (in summary of course) of the gospel—God's love and Jesus's sacrificial death. But Ferguson notes this statement implies that God's love for me hinges on what Jesus has done for me. In

---

8. Ferguson, *Whole Christ*, 80.
9. Ferguson, *Whole Christ*, 64.

other words, God doesn't *want* to love me, but because of Jesus, somehow God now *must* love me.[10] As if God holds his nose as he welcomes us into the family. Ferguson suggests that once that vision of God takes root in our hearts and in our churches, it is difficult to overcome.[11] But that is not the story of the gospel. Perhaps the best-known passage in all of Scripture, John 3:16, tells us just the opposite: "For God so loved the world that he sent his only Son."[12] Jesus's life and death and resurrection is the outworking *from* God's love not the cosmic bribe *for* God's love.

At its essence, the judgmental, suffocating, controlling version of church that tells people what to think, how to live, whom to vote for, what to wear, and whom to associate with is a misguided attempt to protect God. As if God can't handle being associated with real people and so the attempt is to create fake ones. Grace is a scandal. And churches don't like scandals. Unwittingly, in attempting to hide the scandal of grace, we too often make scandals of our own. I cannot help but think of the mayor in the movie *Chocolat* who condemns any hint of pleasure. He persecutes the new chocolatier who has set up shop in town (in the middle of Lent no less) only to eventually sneak into her shop and gorge himself on truffles and cakes and is found the next morning hungover on sweets, passed out in the shop window—dis-graced.

The beauty of *The Brothers K*, however, is not found in Duncan's depiction of the church, as cathartic as it is to dislike the church leadership's actions or as humorous as the Chance boy's childhood rebellion often is. The beauty is in Duncan's unwillingness to oversimplify. It would have been easy to write a novel decrying the evil and danger of ultra-fundamentalist churches. Instead, Duncan holds out hope. Kincade's brother Irwin, somehow, finds real faith at the church. His faith leads him to become a conscientious objector to the Vietnam War but also to answer the call to duty when the same church lies about his faith to the army recruiters. This same faith leads Irwin to protest the torture and eventual murder of a young Vietnamese soldier. And that same faith makes him unwilling to bow the knee and betray his conscience even when it results in his own torture in the military asylum in California. At the end of the novel, a small band of church misfits, the church within the church, embarks on an RV road trip

10. Ferguson, *Whole Christ*, 64.
11. Ferguson, *Whole Christ*, 64.
12. Ferguson, *Whole Christ*, 66.

from Washington to California to rescue Irwin from the asylum. The same church that split the Chance family is also the church that ends up helping bring them back together.

The Brothers K also exposes the dangers of fundamentalist anything. Kincaid's brother Peter, in rejection of his mother's faith, dives deep into eastern mysticism. He receives a Fulbright scholarship in grad school that allows him to travel to India, believing he is a "displaced Indian seeking an honorable return passage to the East."[13] Hoping to follow in the footsteps of his "only political hero, Mahatma Gandhi,"[14] Peter quickly finds that he can't stomach to ride in the same train as the Untouchable class, nor eat their food. So instead of solidarity with the common people he hides out in libraries behind stacks of books. Duncan summarizes Peter's experience in his typical irreverent and yet poignant prose:

> It was while hunching, clammy-fleshed, with the animals and Untouchables in the aisles of these third-class train cars praying for nothing more transcendent than the strength to hold his anus shut that Peter felt driven to make his first compromise with Mother India: Gandhi or no Ghandi, he would henceforth do his traveling in first-class, glassed-in, air-conditioned train cars equipped with private, flush-toileted bathrooms.
>
> Americanness, he was discovering, is not an easy quality to crucify—at least not without crucifying the entire American.[15]

Peter's convictions give way when reality gets complicated. Air conditioning and indoor plumbing turn out to be desirable modern conveniences.

Kincaid's oldest brother Everett's rejection of the family faith leads him to take on the persona of the prototypical university radical. He writes leftist political diatribes for the University of Washington's student newspaper, dodges the draft, and flees to Canada. But ultimately, he ends up not believing everything he writes, he just knows how to push the right buttons and get a crowd riled up. For all his glory as a university hero he finds himself alone, in exile. The stifling certainty of the Washougal SDA church is replaced with the dogmatic renunciations of Peter's Eastern spirituality and Everett's activist hippy-ism, and they fall just as flat. Duncan does not allow for easy answers.

13. Duncan, *Brothers K*, 412.
14. Duncan, *Brothers K*, 413.
15. Duncan, *Brothers K*, 413.

All Swirling and Weaving

A telling interaction occurs between Everett and one of the University of Washington professors. Dr. Gurtzner, a history professor, confesses to the students that like most of them he "opposes the American military presence in Vietnam" but he does not consider himself a revolutionary. He then explains why:

> In order to become a true revolutionary . . . you must first of all jettison your ability to recall or honor the complexities of a nuanced historic or personal past. More details explain things more, but less details confuse things less, and a leader out to galvanize thousands of zealous followers must consistently shun complexity, even at the cost of lucidity and truth.[16]

This seems to be the heart of Duncan's objection with the church—shunning complexity to galvanize followers at the expense of truth. And to truth, I think he would add wonder and beauty and joy.[17] It is not only that the stringent dogmatism of the church leaves little room for doubts or mystery or grace, but it also severs any connection between God and the goodness of the world.

One of my favorite moments in the novel is Kincaid's description of Brother Beal's home run at summer church camp. Beal, the youth pastor, had played college baseball and to impress Sister Durrel (another youth worker in the church) he hit a whopping home run during the church softball game. As he rounded the bases, he transitioned from the typical home run trot to a dance. Kincaid describes it like this:

> He wasn't running bases at all. He was *dancing* them. Our first reaction was to gawk. There stood our big pious weenie of a Sabbath School teacher on second base, eyes closed, body motatin', zonked face impossibly unembarrassed as his hands mojoed a solo on a sax no more visible than the Holy Ghost. . . . But what really won me over was his butt. What finally made it impossible for me not to like the man was how right there on the Adventist basepaths, right in front of eighty or ninety of the kind of pious adult spectators who spent their every Sabbath if not their entire lives trying to forget the existence of things like butts, Beal's buns were trying to light a friction inside his jeans; they were gyrating like a washing machine with its load off balance; they were thrashing his pants like two big halibuts against the bottom of a boat. And the

---

16. Duncan, *Brothers K*, 316.

17. I'm thinking here in particular of an essay by Duncan called "Wonder, Yogi, Gladly" in *God Laughs and Plays*, 5–16.

They Did Indeed Move in a Mysterious Way

wonderful thing, the amazing thing, was how once his older audience got over the shock of it, they began to look amused at, then fascinated by, and finally downright grateful toward his writhing reminder that yes buns did exist, and yes, every one of us owned not one but two of the things, and yes, like the God who created them in His image, they did indeed move in a mysterious way.[18]

For a fleeting moment, Brother Beal's homerun and gyrating trip around the base pads reintroduced joy into the Washougal SDA church family. It also makes Kincaid "all the sadder" to see Beal quickly transform back into the stiff-collared, lifeless teacher at Sabbath school. The story the church was telling wasn't big enough to include both the glory of God and the glory of squaring up a fastball with the barrel of a bat, let alone a celebratory dance around the bases.

Duncan appears allergic to anything resembling doctrinal certainty. I understand his aversion, but I believe there is some certainty that exists within the faith that we need to hold onto. Certainty and fundamentalism are not exactly synonymous. I'm a confessing Presbyterian. I may be the only human alive that still gets choked up every time I ask and answer the first question of the Heidelberg Catechism. I believe in God, the Father Almighty, and in Jesus Christ his only Son our Lord. I also read the Gospel narratives and see that Jesus spends a significant amount of his time blowing up the certainty of the religious establishment of his day. But isn't it possible to hold to a certainty that opens the world up instead of closes it?

In his essay "Wonder, Yogi, Gladly" Duncan claims that he has "lived a faith life rich in rivers, poor in church services."[19] Again, I understand what he means; for three years I lived in Cooke City, Montana, with Soda Butte Creek and the Lamar River in my backyard. I also lament that Duncan hasn't found a richness in both the natural world and the life of a congregation. I believe in a God whose imagination created aardvarks and banana slugs and a whole pallet of greens and yellows on the dappled sides of a Yellowstone cutthroat trout. I have also been in sanctuaries where everyone in the room experienced that same God's presence—even Presbyterian sanctuaries.

When we are getting the story right the membership leaves the Sunday worship or the midweek bible study or the pastoral counseling chair

---

18. Duncan, *Brothers K*, 71.
19. Duncan, *God Laughs*, 6.

feeling lighter, freer, and the world becomes larger, not smaller. I have a quote by David Hansen on my desk that I read most weeks before I get up to preach that says, "Jesus will bear their burdens if only I can bear Jesus to them."[20] I don't always succeed, and God is gracious in my failures.[21] But this is the goal: to give to Jesus what he longs to take—our sins and sufferings—and to reawaken our creative imagination as ambassadors of God created in his image.

I believe the two parts to this goal are related. When God is miser and killjoy, making his list and checking it twice, all our energy is spent on self-analysis and perception control, instead of actually living. The story the Washougal SDA Church is telling in *The Brothers K* shrinks the world. Fear becomes the dominant motivation instead of love. God becomes the heavenly school Principal you want to avoid instead of the welcoming Father with wide open arms. The world becomes riddled with dangers instead of wonders to explore. The gospel tells a better story.

---

20. Hansen, *Art of Pastoring*, 142.

21. This is perhaps the best argument for a well-thought-out liturgy of worship and theologically rich singing—even when the preacher misses the gospel in the sermon, the shape of the service still proclaims it.

The World Was All Before Them, Such as It Was

Marilynne Robinson's *Jack*

> "Dear Lord, bless these gifts to our use and us to Thy service, and keep us ever mindful of the needs of others. Amen."
>
> "I've always objected to that prayer. If it were only a little easier to know what they are. The needs of others. A good deal more is required than just being mindful."
>
> Marilynne Robinson, HOME

MARILYNNE ROBINSON'S LATEST NOVEL, *Jack*, begins with a seventy-page conversation between Jack Boughton and his eventual wife, Della Miles. They are locked in the Bellefontaine Cemetery in St. Louis in the middle of the night. It is one year after their first date—a date that was cut short when Jack was chased out of the restaurant by debt collectors. From Robinson's previous novels we already know Jack and Della eventually have a common-law marriage and a child. We also know that they separate. We know that their marriage is complicated, not simply because Jack is an alcoholic and a drifter but because he is White, and Della is Black, during a time in Missouri when anti-miscegenation laws were strictly enforced. We know they met when Jack walked her home in the rain because he saw her drop some of her school papers and offered to help.

We know nothing of Jack and Della's courtship; Robinson introduces it with seventy pages of dialogue. Many conversations these days don't even involve audible words let alone full sentences with punctuation and subtle allusions to Milton and Shakespeare. Writing dialogue is a particular kind of skill. Writing seventy pages of one conversation is a marvel.

Reading a sentence from Marilynne Robinson reminds me of an Irish pub (not in Ireland) I used to frequent that had quotes of well-known Irish literary figures painted on the walls. My favorite was attributed to Oscar Wilde and read, "I spent all morning taking out a comma and all afternoon putting it back." Every word in Robinson's novel is placed exactly where it needs to be.

Jack regularly quotes Milton and Shakespeare and Scripture, and Robinson rarely gives the reference. She either assumes her readers will notice or she is indifferent to whether they recognize the reference or not. Nods to Calvin, Hart Crane, Paul Dunbar, H. D., and *The Dream of the Rood* make their way into Jack's thoughts or as subtle allusions in his conversations. Robinson is working in the shadow of a great cloud of witnesses.

Midway through the novel, Della writes Jack a letter about returning home to Memphis to try to smooth over their relationship with her family. She addresses the letter "Dear Friend." Upon reading it, Jack notes to himself that she did not say, "While I think on thee."[1] At first, I kept reading on to find out what the letter *did* say. Then I realized that "While I think on thee" must be a quote from some source and a quick search revealed it was from Shakespeare's "Sonnet 30."

"Sonnet 30" is about remembering past losses and feeling the pain afresh. The sonnet is rather depressing until the concluding couplet: "But if the *while I think on thee, dear friend,* / All losses are restor'd, and sorrows end."[2] Shakespeare's sonnet is a lament that ends with hope. Della's letter does not. Robinson uses this subtle allusion in a brief aside in Jack's thought process, one many readers probably never notice (how many people have "Sonnet 30" memorized?), to increase the weight of the pain of Jack's life. Those who have read the other Gilead books know that not all losses for Jack will be restored, and his life is often sorrow upon sorrow.

At the end of the novel, Jack and Della are on the same bus leaving Memphis to an unknown future together. But because of Jim Crow they are not able to sit together. Robinson uses a well-known Milton reference to close their story. She writes, "They were together, after their fashion, and

---

1. Robinson, *Jack*, 180.
2. Shakespeare, *Sonnets*, 30; my italics.

the world was all before them, such as it was."³ The world was all before them, such as it was. Such as it is. Unlike Adam and Eve leaving Eden in *Paradise Lost,* Jack and Della can't even hold hands as they set off into their own exile.

In a review blurb on the back cover of *Jack,* Mark Athitakis suggests, "Marilynne Robinson is so powerful a writer that she can reshape how we read." I am not sure of the context in which he suggests this, but I agree with the statement as it stands.⁴ Robinson's style forces me to read and reread. It is not simply for the beauty of each sentence but her ability to capture the intensity and humanity and depth of a moment. Often with the sparsest exposition.

Robinson includes little about Jack's mother in all four Gilead novels. Jack didn't return home for her funeral after his time in prison. She was already deceased at the time of the events in *Home,* the novel that deals primarily with the Boughton family. However, in a tangential paragraph prompted by a few thoughts about the onset of autumn, Robinson digs into layers of relationship. Jack's train of thought shifts from awareness of the days getting colder in St. Louis to his childhood in Iowa and how often he was out of the house, even in the depths of winter. Then Jack flashes back:

> He could feel the relief in the house [when he returned home], but they had learned not to ask where he had been, what he had been up to. Even Teddy. They were grateful that he was in out of the cold. His mother would come into the kitchen to put his supper on the table and pour his milk.
>
> "You never talk about your mother."
> "Yes, I don't."
>
> That tremor in her hands. He could have said, "I found a little creek where the ice wasn't solid yet, panes of ice, clear as glass." He could even say he liked the sound they made under his boots, how they shattered when he threw them down. She knew about his interest in fragile things and would have liked to hear that for once no harm was done. But she was fragile, so he could not bring himself to comfort her. Half the time he would roll up whatever he could of his supper in a piece of bread and be out the door again. Better the cold. Better the dark. Why was that? He knew how she

---

3. Robinson, *Jack,* 309; my italics.
4. I was unable to locate the full review.

felt when he left. He felt it himself. Dear Jesus, keep me harmless. He knew what that meant. Keep me alone.[5]

It is a devastating image: a lone boy shattering sheets of ice on the banks of a river and his early intuition that it was best for the family for him to be gone, out of the way. To be harmless was to be alone. When he comes in out of the cold, he *doesn't* tell his mother what he was doing. Her hands tremble. Jack doesn't speak. Robinson phrases it, "He could have said." But he didn't. Jack's intuition was mistaken. Even in his absence he caused harm. I didn't intend to reread the other Gilead books this summer, but after reading *Jack* I was curious to see how often Jack was referenced in the other stories. He is prominently featured in *Gilead* and in *Home*, but even when he is gone, he is on everyone's mind. One could make the argument that Jack is the main character of the entire series. But his presence is subtle, estranged. He is absent from Gilead for twenty years, but he is always there in the worries of his family.

Robinson's writing has the power to reshape how we read. I believe she can also help reshape how we pastors, pastor. I read an interview with comedian Jerry Seinfeld several years ago in which he confessed that sometimes he would work on a particular bit in his stand-up routine for over a decade. He would obsess over the phrasing, the timing, getting the description just right. He would agonize over it, practice it, revise it, and then he would finally use it, only to edit it again.[6]

The art of pastoring is no different. Those of us who preach weekly have to consider phrasing and timing and delivery. But what I have in mind is not simply our diction during sermon preparation or writing style in newsletter articles. We are called to *care for people* as much as Robinson cares for words or Seinfeld cares for punchlines.

The question is, how? What does care for people look like practically? Near the end of Robinson's second Gilead installment, *Home*, Reverend Boughton, Jack, and his sister Glory sit down for chicken and dumplings. The aging Boughton asks Glory to bless the meal. She prays a familiar family prayer: "Dear Lord, bless these gifts to our use and us to Thy service, and keep us ever mindful of the needs of others. Amen." Boughton responds, "Yes, I've always objected to that prayer. If it were only a little easier to know

---

5. Robinson, *Jack*, 85.
6. See Weiner, "Jerry Seinfeld."

what they are. The needs of others. A good deal more is required than just being mindful. That has certainly been my experience."[7]

A good deal more is required than just being mindful of others' needs. One of the lingering questions that threads its way through Robinson's Gilead series is the question, What help does Jack need? No answer is given. Nobody knows. Not his father or Reverend Ames. Not his family. Jack doesn't seem to have any idea. Repeatedly he acknowledges that he doesn't know why he is the way he is. Though he routinely apologizes for it. During Jack and Della's midnight walk through the cemetery he says to her, "I aspire to utter harmlessness. It's a contest I have with myself. I have no real aptitude for harmlessness, which makes it interesting."[8]

Jack is a thief even from a young age. He didn't know why. He never stole out of need. Most of the things he would take were useless to him, they weren't things he even wanted. He is a drinker where oblivion seems to be the goal. He had a child with a young girl, he was in college, she was still a teenager. He abandoned them both and never met his daughter. The baby died young from a fever. Jack left home for twenty years. Near the end of *Home*, he is overwhelmed with the guilt and the loss of Della, and he attempts to kill himself with the fumes of his father's old car in the barn in which he used to hide. His suicide attempt fails, and he leaves days before his father dies, unable or unwilling to be there when his siblings come home for the service. He has "no real aptitude for harmlessness."

Much of what used to fall under the heading of pastoral care has been farmed out to other professions. Counseling, therapy, twelve-step groups, rehab, yoga, sports clubs, psychiatrists, and life coaches now fill this role. These have their place. Utilizing the expertise of a variety of disciplines is only wise. But ultimately, it is Jesus who cures souls and Jesus is left out of most approaches to personal transformation—even within the church.

My seminary education equipped me to slow down and read Scripture in the original languages. It trained me to track through Paul's sentence structure and recognize Hebrew poetry's parallelism. Theology professors introduced me to the character of God, the nature of sin, the glory of salvation. Preaching professors endured early attempts at sermons. I am grateful for all of it. But I only took one course on counseling, and the entirety of pastoral care was a few lectures in a catch-all course that included wedding planning, funerals, how to lead a board meeting, and whether or not to eat

---

7. Robinson, *Home*, 280.
8. Robinson, *Jack*, 61.

All Swirling and Weaving

the cookies offered during home visits. (The conundrum being if I accept some offers but turn down others, some members might be offended. My professor's advice was either eat them all or decline them all.) I learned how to exegete a sentence in Greek but not how to exegete the life of a church member.

In some ways this is inevitable. Each person in my congregation is unique. Their lives have been shaped by a complex set of circumstances, decisions, sufferings, and successes. Life experience, background, trauma, education, family structure—all of the daily details that make up a life are important and formative. But none of it is determinative. You can't plug a person's life events into a computer and print out a conclusive result of what makes them tick or understand how they put their world together. And you certainly can't predict how they will respond to any given situation. As Brian Doyle observes, there is an "incalculable ocean of stories just in [one] town."[9] I would make the same claim, an incalculable ocean of stories can be found in one congregation.

In *Jack*, Robinson is helping me learn how to exegete a life. Exegete is perhaps not the right word. In Biblical exegesis I parse words. I (used to) diagram sentences. I print out the passage on a sheet of paper and I mark it up. I circle repeated words and phrases. I underline the central idea. I triple underscore conjunctions. I spend one good hour with just the words of the passage. I write down every question I can think of as I read and reread the text. Then, I get the general historical background, the immediate literary context, and place the passage into the greater narrative arc of the whole Bible. I find allusions to other parts of Scripture. If I'm in one of Paul's letters I try to map the logical flow of his train of thought. I notice what I notice. Then I pick up commentaries and other reference books to find out what other people have noticed over the years.

This process is not the end of sermon preparation. I have lots of quotes and ideas and circled words and questions and more questions. And a few answers. But I don't have a sermon yet. The congregation finds me competent if I bring some of this study into the pulpit. Much of it is interesting. Some weeks, interesting and competent are the best I can offer. But if it is to truly become a sermon, something mysterious happens between the exegesis and the preaching event. I forget who I heard first call the sermon an event. It is an apt description. It is not just a talk. It is not a lecture. I'm not delivering a paper each week. Sometimes it's that; maybe, most of the

---

9. Doyle, *Mink River*, 13.

time it's that. But on occasion, when I stand up with the Bible in my hand and proclaim to the best of my ability the message of the passage, the reality of God-with-us becomes so apparent that everyone in the room feels his presence. This mystery, I trust, is the work of the Spirit.

When it comes to holding and caring for the stories of our members as pastors, shepherding is closer to this in-between mystery of the work of the Spirit than it is to exegesis. I do need to know facts about people. Historical background, current life situations and circumstances, a general sense of their families of origin are all helpful. But the base facts of Jack's life do not tell the story that Robinson is trying to tell. Jack is the son of a Presbyterian pastor. He is a thief. He is an alcoholic. For employment, he stocks shoes in a failing shoe store, teaches dancing lessons, and washes dishes. He is a drifter, a ne'er-do-well. He has been to prison. He fathered a child out of wedlock and then abandoned the mother and his daughter. He doesn't go home for his own mother's funeral. He is White, in Missouri, in the 1950s.

If you look at that list of the facts about Jack's life, it is hard to blame Della's family for not wanting their daughter involved with him. When you read the story, however, you desperately want things to work out for them. Why? Because he is more than just the details of his life. He is kind. He is literary. He is much further along in the question of race than his father, or Ames, or the whole town of Gilead, Iowa. He is winsomely self-deprecating. He is loved. But he is more than these things too. Jack is not beyond the reach of grace. I want the story of Jack in the stories of Gilead to be about hope and not loss. This must be the heart of the church.

Jack is surrounded by pastors. But it is only Della who is able to bring about any reform in his life. After their seventy-page midnight conversation in the cemetery, Jack begins to reflect on how Della is shaping him:

> Della was speaking to him sometimes in his thoughts, or she was quiet, simply there at the edge of his vision. In her gentle way she was making everything easier. What would she find becoming in him? That was what he did. And by putting himself in the way of survival, not to put too fine a point on it, he was doing as she had asked him to do, so forthrightly. Can these bones live? Oh, Lord, you know. But for you, Miss Miles, I am eating this sandwich, for you I am smiling at this stranger, for you I am trying to sleep.[10]

Can these bones live? I wonder if that is not the question Robinson is wrestling with in the entire novel, perhaps the entire Gilead series. It is

10. Robinson, *Jack*. 83.

All Swirling and Weaving

another allusion to a biblical reference, Ezekiel 37, and the valley of dry bones. It is the Old Testament version of the promise of new birth, of restoration and renewal. Can the valley of dry bones come back to life? Can Jack?

How is grace extended to someone who refuses to accept it? Della's love is a costly love. It costs her her reputation. Her job. Her family. It potentially will take from her the already stunted "freedom" she has in the Jim Crow segregation of St. Louis. And there is no assurance of the success of this sacrifice, what Tolkien calls, "hope with no guarantees."[11]

When we get to their story in *Home*, Della and Jack have separated. She gave up everything and still ended up raising their son alone. This is the love I am inviting my congregants into. This is the grace we are called to extend: a laying down of our lives with no guarantee of success. But with the resilient conviction that God might be at work still. The courage to hope that the mystery of the Spirit might blow again, someday. It is a hard bargain, I know. We want results. We want to see transformation. We want dry bones to come back to life. But the Spirit is not at our beck and call. "Can these bones live? Oh, Lord, you know."

As a pastor, part of my job is to hold tightly to the reality that whenever two people gather, Jesus is also there. In the typical counseling relationship, we think of the therapist and the patient. Two people—one presumed to be competent and trained and the other in some sort of need. But in any pastoral conversation it is never just the pastor and the parishioner. A third person is present.[12] Jesus is at work in the pastor and the parishioner. Two people, both in need, and a third, Jesus, who is extravagant in his provision, the wonderful counselor. We rarely pay this attention. It is hard to imagine what it might mean to pay attention to this.

Eugene Peterson believed that one of the adjectives that should be used to describe pastors is *subversive*. He says he didn't like being considered "nice but insignificant."[13] He often imagined the successful businessman shaking his hand in the greeting line after the Sunday morning sermon and

---

11. Tolkien to Michael Straight, undated (editor notes, "probably January or February 1956"), in *Letters*, 255.

12. I was reminded of this in a lecture by David Powlison in the course Dynamics of Biblical Change at the Christian Counseling and Education Foundation.

13. Peterson, *Contemplative*, 27.

saying, "This was wonderful, Pastor, but now we have to get back to the real world, don't we?"[14] Peterson notes,

> Then I remember that I am a subversive. My long-term effectiveness depends on my not being recognized for who I really am. If he (the businessman) realized that I actually believe the American way of life is doomed to destruction, and that another kingdom is right now being formed in secret to take its place, he wouldn't be at all pleased. If he knew what I was really doing and the difference it was making, he would fire me.
>
> Yes, I believe that. I believe that the kingdoms of this world, American and Venezuelan and Chinese, will become the kingdom of our God and Christ, and I believe this new kingdom is already among us. That is why I'm a pastor, to introduce people to the real world and train them to live in it.[15]

More is at work than we can see. A better kingdom is coming and already here. As Peterson concludes, that is why we pastor. We are introducing people to the real world.

A few years ago, I came across a similar thought in Darrell Johnson's book *The Glory of Preaching*. I typed it out and taped it to the pulpit in our sanctuary so that I could read it every week before I preached. Johnson writes,

> You the preacher know something about every person sitting or standing before you that they may or may not know. You know that, having been made by God, the only way to live is his way. You know that, having been made for him, only he can finally fulfill all their longings. Indeed, you know that all their longings are symptomatic of their longings for him. . . . That is, you know that nothing less than Jesus himself will ever satisfy them. Again, they may not know this. And you do not necessarily need to tell them all this at once. But you know this mystery. And, therefore, you speak to them in this mystery.[16]

Jesus is everywhere in the story of *Jack*. A few weeks after finishing the novel, I picked up my copy of the book one morning and read a few pages. Jack constantly uses the phrase, "sweet Jesus" or "dear Jesus" in his thoughts. When he first visits Della's house, he notices the picture of Jesus

---

14. Peterson, *Contemplative*, 27.
15. Peterson, *Contemplative*, 27.
16. Johnson, *Preaching*, 234–35.

on her piano—the only picture in color. Several times throughout the novel he references the picture. When Jack is completely lost, he finds himself walking into a Black church on a Sunday morning. He stays for rice and beans and plays a few hymns on the piano in the church basement. He begins regular meetings with the pastor, Reverend Hutchinson. Jack's father is a pastor. His godfather, Reverend Ames, is a pastor. His father-in-law, Reverend Miles, is a pastor. And yet, Jack still cannot make their faith his own. Can these bones live?

I thought this chapter was going to be about why the prodigals in our lives are often so compelling. Jack is infuriating to his family and yet they all feel drawn to helping him. Burley Coulter in Wendell Berry's Port William series is a loveable scoundrel with a penchant to drink too much and disappear to his fishing cabin instead of facing life's hardships. We love prodigals and underdogs. Partly, I think, because we all have a sense of our own prodigality. We want (need?) to believe that people can change. Or that God can change them. And us.

Upon finishing *Jack*, I thought through what Robinson's life work—the fictional Iowa town of Gilead—was ultimately about. Loss. Grace. Forgiveness. Redemption. Patience. Family. Race. Misunderstanding. Competing responsibilities. Costly love. It is all of these. And more. The Gilead series invites a lifetime of reading. This chapter could have gone in a variety of directions. I keep coming back to hope.

Robinson maps Jack onto the story of the prodigal son. He leaves Gilead for the far country and eventually comes home. Glory, the dutiful sister, is much more generous than the older brother in Jesus's story. When I reread *Home* after reading *Jack*, I now had the backstory of Jack and Della's marriage. It only made the ending of *Home* more excruciating. After twenty years in the far country Jack returns to Gilead. Alone. Without Della or their son, Robert. He attempts to be helpful. He restores the place to how it was when they were all younger. Glory appreciates having someone besides their father for company. But he keeps her distant. He is waiting, hoping to hear a word from Della. "She has forgiven so much, he said."[17] Could she possibly forgive more? And then a few days before his father dies and a few days before Della and Robert come to Iowa to find him, Jack leaves, again. On his final day at home, Robinson writes,

> The day passed. Glory wanted to value it, though of course she could not enjoy it. She would probably never see her brother

---

17. Robinson, *Home*, 324.

again—in this life, as Teddy had said. Sweet Jesus, she thought, love this thief, too.[18]

Sweet Jesus, love this thief, too. This is an allusion to the thief on the cross next to Jesus at his crucifixion. Before he dies, Jesus promises him that "today, you will be with me in paradise."[19] And right here is the basis for all of our hope. The deep, deep love of Jesus.

This is what keeps me going as a pastor. The promise that God is not finished with us yet, with anyone. The promise that at any given moment, a turn of a phrase in a sermon, or a verse in a well-worn hymn, or a smile and a warm bowl of soup, might be the moment when the love of Jesus becomes real in a someone's life. Might be the moment when the lights suddenly turn on and eyes are opened, and a lifetime of clouds begin to roll away. Not love as an idea, or a doctrine, but the tangible experience that changes everything. Make these bones live.

The end of *Home* is chronologically the last scene of the Gilead series. *Jack* was written last but acts as a prequel to the other books. Part of me hopes that Robinson has one more novel in her. I want a good ending for Della and Jack. But there is something in the ache for that desire that is truer to life and to the pastoral call. In the final scene, Glory imagines that someday Jack's son might return to Gilead:

> She thought, Maybe this Robert will come back someday. Young men are rarely cautious. What of Jack will there be in him? . . . He will be curious about the place, though his curiosity will not override his good manners. He will talk to me a little while, too shy to tell me why he has come, and then he will thank me and leave, walking backward a few steps, thinking. Yes, the barn is still there, yes, the lilacs, even the pot of petunias. This was my father's house. And I will think, He is young. He cannot know that my whole life has come down to this moment.
>
> That he has answered his father's prayers.
>
> The Lord is wonderful.[20]

The Lord is wonderful, even in the ache. Even in the "maybe." Maybe Jack's son will come back. Glory doesn't know. Maybe Robinson doesn't even know. But the hope is enough to keep me going.

---

18. Robinson, *Home*, 315.
19. This is another allusion to Scripture, Luke 23:43.
20. Robinson, *Home*, 324–25.

Playful Excess

Andrew Peterson's *The Wingfeather Saga*

As long as God remembers us, who we are will remain.
John Swinton, Dementia: Living in the Memories of God

It would be a stretch to say the reason we had children was to read them books. But that hope was near the top of the list. The first story I read to Addie when she got home from the hospital was *Dawdle Duckling*. That was sixteen years ago. It became a favorite, for all of us. I can still find the rhythm: "But the fourth little duckling dawdles and dreams, preens and plays, splashes and spins, dunks and dips. 'Quack! Catch up!' says Mama Duck.'" And then Dawdle's defiant answer, "NO! Quack! Quack! I won't catch up."[1] Addie is not a dawdler. I wish she would make more time to splash and spin. She does spend lots of time preening in front of the bathroom mirror these days. She has remained a reader. She requested several books for her sweet-sixteen birthday. They're cheaper than a car.

Before the kids were old enough for school, we would read at nap time and before bed (and often before dinner for good measure). It provided routine for the kids and for us. Our dog, Boswell, would join us in the kids' room. He became as familiar with the word *story-time* as he was with the word *walk*. We read widely. Mo Willems, Sandra Boynton, Dr. Suess, *Goodnight Moon*, *Winnie the Pooh*, *Ferdinand*, *Where the Wild Things Are*, *The Shrinking of Treehorn*, *The Jesus Storybook Bible*, and *The Oxcart Man* were all worn thin. When we flew from Washington to my parents' house in Iowa

---

1. Buzzeo, *Dawdle Duckling*, 20–23.

Playful Excess

for Christmas and summer vacation, my mom took over story-time. Jackson always requested *Tacky the Penguin* and Mom always obliged; she used a nasally, high-pitched voice for Tacky's singing and Jackson would laugh every time. Moving from board books to picture books to chapter books always brought excitement tinged with sadness, especially with Isaac, our youngest. When would we read these stories again?

This year, Isaac and I worked our way through Andrew Peterson's *Wingfeather Saga*. Peterson is best known for his music. He is a storytelling singer-songwriter. My brother and sister-in-law introduced us to Peterson's *Behold the Lamb of God* Christmas concert, and it has become a sacred ritual in our household each December. I have long been drawn to storytelling in music—Bruce Springsteen, Simon and Garfunkel, Rich Mullins. I played my parents' LP of *Peter, Paul and Mary Live* repeatedly as a child and memorized all the stories they told between each song. When we discovered Peterson had a book series, we put it on our family read-aloud list. *The Wingfeather Saga* is a four-volume, epic-style fantasy story with a whimsical tone. Peterson described his project as the *Princess Bride* meets *Lord of the Rings*.

We read the first volume, *On the Edge of the Dark Sea of Darkness*, together as a whole family six years ago, but our middle child, Jackson, could no longer abide our plodding, one-chapter-a-night pace, so he finished the other three books without us. I was proud of his initiative, but I missed sharing the stories with him. I saved my reading of the series until Isaac was old enough to read it with me.

Lately our read-aloud time has been haphazard. With the kids' sports and church meetings and Cubs games it doesn't always happen outside of a quick chapter at bedtime. When it does, we read in the living room because we're all less likely to fall asleep out there. I try to use different voices for the characters. Isaac appreciates it; Katie laughs at me. I doubt Audible will be calling anytime soon. My father, Jay, joined us almost every night before making his way back to his room. When he moved in with us, I wasn't sure how stories would work for him. He often recalls details from decades ago but usually by two o'clock he can't remember what we had for lunch. Regularly, however, he would ask if we were "reading Janner and Tink [the two main characters] tonight?"

It took me a while to warm up to Peterson's style. Both *The Princess Bride* (the movie) and *The Lord of the Rings* (the books) are favorites of mine. But the combination of goofy and epic took some getting used to.

All Swirling and Weaving

Peterson's world of Skree is occupied by giant lizards with poisonous saliva called Fangs. The Fangs are from a land called Dang across the Dark Sea of Darkness and are known as the Fangs of Dang. They are led by Gnag the Nameless. The story begins with a black carriage riding into the town of Glipwood in the middle of the night. The carriage kidnaps a young girl, Sara Cobbler, and takes her away. We don't hear from Sara Cobbler again until book two. The narrator tells us, "Sara's parents had held a funeral wake for her. Being carried off by the Black Carriage was like dying. It could happen to anyone, at any time, and there was nothing to be done about it but to hope the Carriage kept moving when it rattled down your lane."[2] It is an ominous opening. Peterson introduces his epic where he is most comfortable—with a song:

> Lo, beyond the River Blapp
> The Carriage comes, the Carriage Black
> By shadowed steed with shadowed tack
> And shadowed driver driving
>
> Child, pray the Maker let you sleep
> When comes the Carriage down your street
> Lest all your dreams be dreams of teeth
> And Carriages arriving
>
> To wrest you from your berth and bower
> In deepest night and darkest hour
> Across the sea to frozen tower
> Where Gnag the Nameless pounds you.[3]

From the start, the reader knows that the world of Skree is a land of shadow. Peterson's lyrical introduction to the Black Carriage alerts parents that the story they are about to read will not gloss over pain and loss. The Iggiby children—Janner, Tink, and Leeli—know that their little town of Glipwood is controlled by the Fangs. They know their father was killed in the uprising. They know the warning in the song of the Carriage Black, with shadowed tack and shadowed driver driving. But they don't know the whole story yet. Or their role in it.

I've always been intrigued by how writers of children's books choose to reveal the heartaches of the world. Traditional fairytales had no qualms about introducing dark subject matter. Original versions of the big bad wolf in *Little Red Riding Hood* have the wolf eating both Grandma and Red.

---

2. Peterson, *Dark Sea*, 10.
3. Peterson, *Dark Sea*, 7–8.

Playful Excess

Harry Potter's parents are killed by Voldemort. Orphans abound in children's literature—from *Oliver Twist* and *Huckleberry Finn* to *Anne of Green Gables*, the *Boxcar Children* and *Peter Pan* to *Matilda* and *Harry Potter*, and pretty much every superhero out there—Superman, Spiderman, Batman, take your pick. Parents are easy to kill off. As much as we might want to protect our children from the shadowy side of life, a regular habit of reading to them doesn't allow it.

The coffee shop I am writing in displays local artwork on the walls. Often these are for sale. This month's exhibit, however, is from Ms. Brophy's first-grade class. From what I can gather, one of her students, Jacob, died this year. The whole class drew pictures of Jacob and wrote out their favorite memories of him. The coffee shop stuck eighteen 8.5 by 11 pages to the interior brick wall with blue painter's tape. The spelling is what you would imagine from first graders with *d*'s meant to be *b*'s and random capitalization.

One student wrote: "My favorite memory with Jacob when we picked flowers." [*sic*]

Another: "I loved being your friend."

Another: "Jacob was my favorite person."

Another: "Jacob's favorite color is blue and my favorite color is blue too."

And: "My favorite thing about Jacob was he loved m&m's." She even drew the ampersand symbol between the *m*'s.

Another: "I liked when he would let me be it, but then think he was it."

Jacob seems to have been an incredible kid. Ms. Brophy was wise to invite her class to process his death and their grief through art and story. Teaching is hard enough. Lord have mercy. The Slow Down coffee shop honored Jacob and his classmates by putting their artwork on the walls. This is the world we bring our kids into—a world where classmates die of cancer and schools practice active shooter drills. At the same time, it is a world where first graders still take delight in sharing a favorite color with a friend. Blue is my favorite too.

Peterson introduces the Iggiby family with Janner, the oldest child, pitching hay in the fields on the morning of the Dragon Day Festival. Tink, the middle son, is up on the roof of their cottage attempting to repair some loose shingles. And Leeli, the youngest, is peeling a bucket of totatoes [*sic*] for their mother, Nia, to use in the stew she is making for supper. The children's grandfather, Podo, lives with them. Podo is out in the garden, Mr.

McGregor style, stopping the thwaps from stealing all their vegetables—thwaps, I guess, are Skree's version of rabbits. The Iggiby's resistance to the Fang's occupation is to carry on with life. Like Jeremiah's instructions to the exiles in Babylon, the Iggibys build a house, plant a garden, make music, and tell their children stories by the fireplace.[4]

The Dragon Day Festival is the Glipwood Township's subversive attempt to remember that things are not the way they are supposed to be. A better world once was and is again possible. The community gathers for games and music and feasting. The Iggibys' chief ally is the bookseller, Oskar N. Reteep. Oskar collects ancient books from before the occupation. Throughout the series Peterson adds ridiculous footnotes referencing these "ancient stories" to give his world a deeper historical background. Here is a footnote referencing *Ridgerunner Rhyme: Poetry of the Mountains* in *On the Edge of the Dark Sea of Darkness*:

> According to Padovan A'Mally's *The Scourge of the Hollow* (Ban Rona, Green Hollows: The Iphreny Group, 3/111), "Ridgerunners are particularly fond of artful verse, though their subject matter is almost exclusively fruit. A free-thinking ridgerunner named Tizrak Rzt scandalized the ridgerunner culture when he composed a poem titled 'Love, Love, Love Hath no Endingness' and famously made no mention of fruit."[5]

The footnote is superfluous. Padovan A'Mally and the Green Hollows Publishing Company are never mentioned again. Ridgerunners do hold a significant role in the story. Their love of fruit provides an enticing motivator for those willing to bribe them for their services. But a footnote about a nonexistent poem scandalizing the ridgerunner community is an example of Peterson's playful excesses. Playful excesses are not superfluous. They are central to the resistance.

In the fall of 1939, shortly after Britain entered World War II, C. S. Lewis preached a sermon titled "Learning in Wartime." Addressing a university audience he begins with the question,

---

4. In Jer 29, the false prophets tell the Israelites that they will be returning to Jerusalem soon and not to worry. Jeremiah gets a different message from the Lord and instructs them to "Build houses and settle down; plant gardens and eat what they produce. Marry and have sons and daughters; find wives for your sons and give your daughters in marriage, so that they too may have sons and daughters. Increase in number there; do not decrease. Also, seek the peace and prosperity of the city to which I have carried you into exile. Pray to the Lord for it, because if it prospers, you too will prosper" (Jer 29:4–7).

5. Peterson, *Dark Sea*, 90.

Playful Excess

> A University is a society for the pursuit of learning. As students, you will be expected to make yourselves, or to start making yourselves into what the Middle Ages called clerks: into philosophers, scientists, scholars, critics, or historians. And at first sight this seems to be an odd thing to do during a great war. What is the use of beginning a task which we have so little chance of finishing? Or, even if we ourselves should happen not to be interrupted by death or military service, why should we—indeed how can we—continue to take an interest in these placid occupations when the lives of our friends and the liberation of Europe are in the balance?[6]

The question is a pointed one. Students were memorizing Latin noun declensions and the atomic structure of chromium while their friends were sailing to France to go off to war. Lewis's answer to his question is to recognize the reality that the world has always been in crisis. "Favorable conditions never come."[7] War accentuates the reality of suffering and our mortality, but these have always been at work in the world. Lewis was neither a pacificist nor an isolationist and recognized that the call to duty for his students might come and if it did, they would be bound to answer. But at that moment, their call was to study. Lewis writes, "If our parents have sent us to Oxford, if our country allows us to remain there, this is *prima facie* evidence that the life which we, at any rate, can best lead to the glory of God at present is the learned life."[8] One phase of the resistance to fascism was for the students and professors in Oxford to continue to read "Tintern Abbey" and *The Mill on the Floss* even as their fellow countrymen headed to war. If such reading matters at all, then it matters whether in times of peace or battle.

In Peterson's world of Skree, the Fangs of Dang terrorized the community. Gnag the Nameless sent out the Black Carriage to kidnap children each night. Their fates were reduced to working as slaves in Gnag's factories or being "transformed" into Fangs themselves for his armies. Yet the folks of Glipwood came together each year on Dragon Day for berry dumplings, lawn games on Dunn's Green, and in hopes of hearing Armulyn the Bard sing songs of ancient Anniera before they all gathered on the cliffs above Fingap Falls to watch the sea dragons. The Iggibys' frustrating daily work in the garden, Oskar's recovery and retelling of the ancient stories, and the

---

6. Lewis, *Weight*, 43.
7. Lewis, *Weight*, 52.
8. Lewis, *Weight*, 49.

annual festivals are all reminders that a larger narrative is at work. Real life continues, even during occupation.

Epic adventures have always gripped me for this reason—they retune my imagination to the reality that my life, most of which is marked by daily routines of work, cooking, busing children to practices, and washing up, is part of something bigger. It is ever-tempting on Sunday mornings for me to despair about what possible good could come of me preaching to the fifty, mostly elderly, members of my congregation yet another sermon based on a passage they have all heard read dozens of times before. How can singing "Be Still My Soul," out of tune and way too slowly, compete with the constant emergency of the daily news cycle?

In college, I was asked to share some reflections on my education at our graduation Baccalaureate service. I mostly talked about friendships I had made over my four years, several of which remain twenty-five years later. I concluded by reading C. S. Lewis's closing paragraph to the Narnia story in *The Last Battle*:

> And as He [Aslan] spoke He no longer looked to them like a lion; but the things that began to happen after that were so great and beautiful that I cannot write them. And for us this is the end of all the stories, and we can most truly say that they all lived happily ever after. But for them it was only the beginning of the real story. All their life in this world and all their adventures in Narnia had only been the cover and the title page: now at last they were beginning Chapter One of the Great Story, which no one on earth has read: which goes on for ever: in which every chapter is better than the one before.[9]

In classic graduation-ceremony melodrama, I looked out over my classmates and told them to consider their life as a story, and to let God be the Author so that they might find their own pages shelved in the great library in heaven. Looking back, it sounds cheesy. Deep down, however, this is still what I believe and what I hope to pass on to my children. We are part of a story that never ends and, as Jonathan Rogers often says, even though it feels like a tragedy we know, ultimately, it is a comedy.[10]

---

9. Lewis, *Last Battle*, 183–84.

10. Like a Shakespearean comedy, history will also end with a wedding; see Rev 21:2. Jonathan Rogers is the host of The Habit podcast. In his interviews, he often refers to the reality that life is a comedy that feels, often, like a tragedy.

When my mother died in 2018, putting together her funeral service was simple enough. She had selected the Scripture and the hymns she wanted years before. She also asked us to read the final paragraph of *The Last Battle*. She must have read the story over thirty times in her lifetime, not a few of those to me. This is why I chose it for my graduation address years before. It was in my bones. My brother Dan volunteered to read it at her service. I am not sure how he got through it. I wouldn't have made it past the first "And."

The death of my mom was my first experience with the loss of someone to whom I was deeply connected. I had lost congregation members whom I loved but I did not have decades of relationship with them. I was the least bereaved person I knew. I am not sure if she was aware she was doing this, but my mother's commitment and delight in reading me stories as a child was secretly preparing me to face death, even her own. My guess is she knew exactly what she was doing. Her life was lived in the grip of a Savior who calls dead people out of graves. She introduced me to Jesus through the epic tales of Narnia and the stories of Walter Wangerin. Reading *The Wingfeather Saga* to Isaac is my attempt to do the same.

Reading to my father and my son at the same time has been an unforeseen gift. I don't remember my dad reading children's books to me. When I was in elementary and middle school, he would wake me up each morning with a glass of orange juice and his Bible. He would read me a chapter of Scripture as I drank the juice before preparing for school. He always brought the orange juice in a yellow, ribbed Tupperware cup. We still have the last of these cups in our own cupboard and it regularly holds his morning orange juice now. When my dad first moved in with us, his doctor described him to me as "pleasantly demented." I am sure this was neither a technical medical term nor politically correct, but I understood what he meant. Unlike many Alzheimer's patients his personality has not changed. He is compliant and happy. He eats whatever we offer him. He watches British crime shows over and again to the point where my children can now quote most of *Father Brown*—all twelve seasons. Storytime, however, is his favorite activity.

At our church in Washington, I witnessed a member deteriorate quickly from Alzheimer's. Carol was a teacher. She specialized in helping children learn to read. She died during the COVID year shortly after we had moved to Iowa, but we watched her memorial service online. Numerous former students had sent in memories about how she patiently sat with them in the hallway or at a table in the Cosmopolis Elementary library and taught them to read. Carol's personality was more affected by her disease than my father's has been. Eventually, her husband was unable to care for her at home. I would visit her once a week in the memory care unit at the nursing home in town. She was often agitated and frustrated. During one visit, I noticed the first *Harry Potter* book on the booster chair in the backseat of our minivan. I brought it with me and read Carol the first chapter. She listened intently; her body relaxed. She laughed at all the right places. I read the next chapter. She was clearly able to follow the storyline. So, I brought it again the next week and read the next few chapters. I don't know if she remembered what had happened in the chapter I read the week before, but it doesn't matter. Week by week we made it through year one at Hogwarts. It clearly calmed and delighted her. In the same way, my dad would laugh each night with us at Peterson's playful excesses.

I recently read John Swinton's book *Dementia*. Swinton teaches practical theology and pastoral care and has served as a psychiatric nurse and mental health chaplain. He reframes how we can think, speak, and act about dementia as followers of Jesus. His subtitle "Living in the Memories of God" grabbed my attention from the start. He does not downplay the horrors of dementia for the person or their caregivers. But he does counter the western assumption of personhood—"I think therefore I am"—with the Biblical promise that God will remember us. Swinton writes,

> Intuitively we feel that there is something very important going on here. "I think therefore I am" is replaced with "We are because God sustains us in God's memory." Our hope lies in the fact that we are living in the memories of God. As long as God remembers us, who we are will remain: "I will not forget you. See, I have engraved you in the palms of my hands" (Isa 49:15–16).[11]

I don't know what my father remembers from moment to moment. Or how he experiences much of life. I can see him tear up each week when my sermon finally (and predictably) makes it to Jesus and his grace. Choir members mention to me that they notice my dad mouthing the words along with them from the pew during the anthem. He still remembers the story in which he is living. If there ever comes a day when he doesn't, I trust God will still remember him.

As I read *The Wingfeather Saga* to Isaac and my father, I sensed that the act of reading this story was a continuation of everything else we do.

---

11. Swinton, *Dementia*, 197.

Playful Excess

Reading isn't an escape. Nor is it superfluous excess. Andrew Peterson can tell such a compelling story because he too knows the expansive story of Scripture. The more in tune with this story we become, the more we see how all of life is somehow integrated—preaching, writing, enjoying live music, evening walks at the end of long summer days, pulling weeds in the garden, serving lunch at the shelter, reading to children and friends with dementia, cross-country skiing through the woods on a still winter day, helping neighbors move their couch. It all swirls and braids and weaves together. An epic story like *The Wingfeather Saga*—it took us eight months to read all four volumes—is able to capture the significance of our daily routines within the framework of the larger story in which we find ourselves.

From January until Easter I always preach a series from one of the four Gospels. I believe in teaching "the whole counsel of God" (Acts 20:27 ESV) but the Gospel narratives keep us centered on the center. For five years I made my way through Matthew's Gospel. Spending four months a year immersed in Matthew for half a decade has been one of the great joys of my life. The New Testament scholar Dale Bruner was my primary guide. He spent a lifetime teaching Matthew to college students and writing a two-volume commentary on the Gospel. His commentary is like none I've ever come across. He is brilliant. He engages, seemingly, with everything that has ever been written in two thousand years on Matthew. Yet his tone is conversational. He often includes anecdotes of conversations with his wife as they went for their evening walk. Reading his commentary feels like you are looking over Bruner's shoulder as he discovers each new insight into the goodness of Jesus. I would use the commentary for my sermon preparation, but it often turned into my own personal devotional time.

In 2020, we moved to Iowa to have my dad move in with us because of his recent diagnosis. We had been at the church in Washington for eleven years. It was the only home, and church, our kids had ever known. We loved the congregation and the community. Saying goodbye was difficult. Saying goodbye during a pandemic felt like betrayal. We had poured our entire lives into the ministry there and God had graciously given us friends and partners that poured into us. We were moving to Iowa without jobs or a home.

After five years of preaching through Matthew, I wanted to finish the Gospel before we left Washington. So, after Easter I pushed on and was able to plan my preaching schedule to have the last verses of Matthew 28 as my final text for my final sermon at First Presbyterian Church of Aberdeen.

115

All Swirling and Weaving

Matthew 28:16-20 includes the great commission to evangelism—"Go therefore and make disciples of all nations" (28:19). And the great call to discipleship making—"Baptizing them in the name of the Father, and the Son and the Holy Spirit, teaching them to obey everything I [Jesus] have commanded you." It was the perfect passage to end on.

We were only four months into a global pandemic. The intensity and chaos of the 2020 election was beginning to ramp up. We were moving to a new city eighteen hundred miles away without any real plan. Katie and I were sad. Our kids were sad and angry. Our denominational process for finding a new pastor averages almost two years, under normal circumstances. I knew I was leaving the congregation in Washington with an arduous journey ahead.

At the end of Matthew 28, Jesus bolsters the great evangelistic commission and the great call to discipleship with a promise: "And behold, I am with you always, to the end of the age." As I prepared that final sermon I read the final pages of Bruner's commentary. It is two volumes—one thousand four hundred seventeen pages. A lifetime of work. As he reflects on Jesus's final words in the Gospel—"I am with you always, to the end of the age"—Bruner's final comment on the book reads,

It means that we will make it.[12]

These were the words I needed to hear, and these were the words I needed to say to the congregation. This is what the Gospel of Matthew and, ultimately, the story of Jesus means. "It means that we will make it."

We will make it. The promise that Jesus is with us always is the promise that God's church will be built, that God's kingdom will come, and that God's will, one day, will be done here on earth in the same way it is in heaven. Perhaps much of the church, as we know it, will need to change before this happens. Certainly, all that we do that mars God's name and character and goodness will be judged or somehow redeemed. The promise that Jesus is with us always is the promise that my father's story will not end even when his memory is completely gone. And that Isaac's life—come what may—will only be a small part of the cover and title page of the Great Story "which goes on for ever: in which every chapter is better than the one before."[13]

12. Bruner, *Churchbook*, 832.
13. Lewis, *Last Battle*, 184.

116

Playful Excess

It turns out reading stories to our kids *is* the reason we had children. This is how the Jesus story continues, in part. Reading books and teaching music, hanging first grade artwork on the walls of neighborhood coffee shops and watching movies, planting vegetables and walking through the woods are all means of taking a stand on hope. One day my father will no longer live with us and Isaac will no longer want me to read to him. Until then, I hope my answer is yes every time one of them asks, "Are we reading tonight?"

Bibliography

Alberta, Tim. "How Politics Poisoned the Evangelical Church." Atlantic, May 10, 2022. https://www.theatlantic.com/magazine/archive/2022/06/evangelical-church-pastors-political-radicalization/629631/.

Anglican Church in North America. *The Book of Common Prayer and the Administration of the Sacraments*. Huntington Beach, CA: Anglican Liturgy, 2019.

Austen, Jane. *Pride and Prejudice*. New York: Penguin Books, 1972.

Barber, Andrew. "Tolkien and the Long Defeat." Gospel Coalition, Dec. 10, 2013. https://www.thegospelcoalition.org/article/tolkien-and-the-long-defeat/.

Barna Group. "Pastors Share Top Reasons They've Considered Quitting Ministry in the Past Year." Apr. 27, 2022. www.barna.com/research/pastors-quitting-ministry/.

Berry, Wendell. *Jayber Crow*. Berkeley: Counterpoint, 2001.

———. *The Memory of Old Jack*. Berkeley: Counterpoint, 1999.

———. *Nathan Coulter*. Berkeley: Counterpoint, 2008.

Bruner, Frederick Dale. *The Churchbook: Matthew 13–28*. Vol. 2 of *Matthew: A Commentary*. Revised ed. Grand Rapids: Eerdmans, 1990.

Buzzeo, Toni. *Dawdle Duckling*. Illustrated by Margaret Spengler. New York: Dial Books for Young Readers, 2003.

Carty, Austin. *The Pastor's Bookshelf: Why Reading Matters for Ministry*. Grand Rapids: Eerdmans, 2022.

Doyle, Brian. *Mink River*. Corvallis, OR: Oregon State University Press, 2010.

Duncan, David James. *The Brothers K*. New York: Bantam, 1992.

———. *God Laughs and Plays: Churchless Sermons in Response to the Fundamentalist Right*. Great Barrington, MA: Triad, 2006.

Emlet, Mike. "Fully Known, Fully Loved." CCEF, Dec. 14, 2021. https://www.ccef.org/fully-known-fully-loved/.

Enger, Leif. *Virgil Wander*. New York: First Grove Atlantic, 2018.

The Episcopal Church. *The Book of Common Prayer and the Administration of the Sacraments and Other Rites and Ceremonies of the Church (1979 Edition)*. Oxford: Oxford University Press, 2005.

Eswine, Zach. *The Imperfect Pastor*. Wheaton, IL: Crossway, 2015.

Faulkner, William. *Requiem for a Nun*. New York: Vintage, 2011.

Ferguson, Sinclair. *The Whole Christ*. Wheaton, IL: Crossway, 2016.

Frost, Michael, and Alan Hirsch. *The Shaping of Things to Come: Innovation and Mission for the 21st-Century Church*. Peabody, MA: Hendrickson, 2003.

Hallström, Lasse, dir. *Chocolat*. Miramax Films, 2000.

Bibliography

Hansen, David. *The Art of Pastoring: Ministry Without All the Answers*. Downers Grove, IL: InterVarsity, 1994.

Hopkins, Gerard Manley. *The Major Works*. Edited by Catherine Phillips. Oxford: Oxford University Press, 1986.

Johnson, Darrell. *The Glory of Preaching*. Downers Grove, IL: InterVarsity, 2009.

Keegan, Claire. *Small Things like These*. New York: Grove, 2021.

Kingsolver, Barbara. *The Bean Trees*. New York: Harper, 1988.

———. *Demon Copperhead*. New York: Harper, 2022.

Lee, Min Jin. *Pachinko*. New York: Grand Central, 2017.

Lewis, C. S. *The Last Battle*. New York: Collier, 1952.

———. *The Screwtape Letters*. New York: Macmillan, 1958.

———. *The Voyage of the Dawn Treader*. New York: Collier, 1952.

———. *The Weight of Glory and Other Addresses*. Grand Rapids: Eerdmans, 1949.

Maclean, Norman. *A River Runs Through It and Other Stories*. Chicago: University of Chicago Press, 1976.

McBride, James. *The Heaven and Earth Grocery Store*. New York: Riverhead, 2023.

McDermott, Alice. *The Ninth Hour*. New York: Picador, 2017.

Melville, Herman. *Moby-Dick*. New York: Bantam, 1981.

Moore, Russell. "Why We Need Fiction for Moral Formation." *The Hutchmoot Podcast*, episode 12. Feb. 1, 2021. https://podcasts.apple.com/us/podcast/russell-moore-why-we-need-fiction-for-moral-formation/id1437192826?i=1000507395035.

Morrison, Toni. *Sula*. New York: Vintage International Edition, 2004.

Peterson, Andrew. *On the Edge of the Dark Sea of Darkness*. Colorado Springs: Waterbrook, 2020.

Peterson, Eugene. *The Contemplative Pastor*. Grand Rapids: Eerdmans, 1989.

———. *Subversive Spirituality*. Grand Rapids: Eerdmans, 1994.

———. *Working the Angles: The Shape of Pastoral Integrity*. Grand Rapids: Eerdmans, 1987.

Plantinga, Cornelius. *Not the Way It's Supposed to Be: A Breviary of Sin*. Grand Rapids: Eerdmans, 1995.

Powlison, David. "The Pastor as Counselor." *Journal of Biblical Counseling* 26 (2012) 23–39.

Robinson, Marilynne. *Home*. New York: Farrar, Straus, and Giroux, 2008.

———. *Jack*. New York: Farrar, Straus, and Giroux, 2020.

Rowling, J. K. *Harry Potter and the Sorcerer's Stone*. New York: Scholastic, 1997.

Salinger, J. D. *The Catcher in the Rye*. Boston: Little, Brown, 1951.

Sayers, Dorothy. *Clouds of Witness*. New York: Harcourt, Brace, 1927.

Shakespeare, William. *The Sonnets*. New York: Barnes and Noble, 1992.

Steinbeck, John. *East of Eden*. New York: Penguin, 1952.

Swinton, John. *Dementia: Living in the Memories of God*. Grand Rapids: Eerdmans, 2012.

Tolkien, J. R. R. *The Fellowship of the Ring*. New York: Houghton Mifflin, 1954.

———. *The Letters of J. R. R. Tolkien*. Edited by Humphrey Carpenter with the assistance of Christopher Tolkien. New York: William Morrow, 2000.

Weiner, Jonah. "Jerry Seinfeld Intends to Die Standing Up." *New York Times Magazine* (December 2012) 24–44.

Williams, Niall. *This Is Happiness*. New York: Bloomsbury, 2019.

Williams, Niall, with Christine Breen. *In Kiltumper: A Year in an Irish Garden*. New York: Bloomsbury, 2021.

Bibliography

Yancey, Philip. *Soul Survivor: How My Faith Survived the Church.* New York: Doubleday, 2001.

———. *Where the Light Fell: A Memoir.* New York: Convergent, 2021.

www.ingramcontent.com/pod-product-compliance
Lightning Source LLC
Chambersburg PA
CBHW070455090426
42735CB00012B/2556